OVERCOMING HURTS & ANGER

Dwight L. Carlson M.D.

Harvest House Publishers
Eugene, Oregon 97402

Cover by PAZ Design, Salem, Oregon

OVERCOMING HURTS AND ANGER
(Revised and Expanded)
Copyright© 2000 by Harvest House Publishers
Eugene, Oregon 97402
www.harvesthousepublishers.com
(First edition published in 1981)

Carlson, Dwight
    Overcoming hurts and anger / Dwight Carlson.—Rev. and expanded.
      p. cm.
    Includes bibliographical references.
    ISBN-13: 978-0-7369-0196-3
    ISBN-10: 0-7369-0196-5
      1. Anger—Religious aspects—Christianity. I. Title.

BV4627.A5.C37 2000
248.8'6—dc21   99-057244

Printed in the United States of America

07 08 09 10 11 12 13 14 / BP / 22 21 20 19 18 17 16 15

With affection to Susan and Greg,
my dear children.

Contents

Preface

I have been a practicing psychiatrist for 25 years, and prior to that, I was a practicing internist for 10 years. During this time I have had the opportunity to care for thousands of patients with every conceivable physical and emotional illness. They have been people from every walk of life, from every social stratum, and from every religious persuasion. One of the most common problems I have encountered among these patients is anger.

This book has been written primarily for the person who has been taught that anger is wrong and doesn't know how to handle anger constructively.

I believe that it is critical for a person to be aware of his own feelings, including anger. Feelings are a valuable guide, a sixth sense, a tool to help us evaluate what is happening around us. Losing our awareness of feelings is as tragic as losing our sense of touch, taste, or smell. Many of us, particularly those of us with religious backgrounds, have been robbed of the right to negative feelings, especially the feeling of anger. This is comparable to a psychological rape, in which a vital part of our humanity is violated, leaving us with irreparable emotional damage. Only when we are aware of our feelings are we able to respond to the inevitable conflicts in life constructively.

Furthermore, so many individuals do not know how to express their feelings, needs, and desires in healthy ways. They either are passive, or in some instances, frankly aggressive, which is a major contributing factor to mishandling anger.

This book offers specific guidelines that can help you deal with hurts and anger. It will teach you how to express your needs and desires in healthy, constructive ways. As a psychiatrist, I believe that anger that is inadequately dealt with is one of the most common problems today. Helping a patient recognize and deal constructively with his hurts and anger is one of the most important things that I can do professionally.

So I was delighted when the publisher of *Overcoming Hurts and Anger* called me and asked if I would update this book. This has given me the opportunity to reevaluate the material for accuracy. Since I originally wrote this 20 years ago, I have seen hundreds of additional patients, taught this material numerous additional times, and have had the opportunity to continue using these principles in my personal life. As I updated this book, I was glad to see that not one major premise needed to be changed. However, a great deal more has been learned by researchers, so I have added new information about the latest research on the devastating effects of unhealthy anger, along with effective treatment strategies.

When I first wrote this book there were two prominent viewpoints being advocated. At one extreme were those who recommended that people give full vent to their anger, sometimes referred to as "ventilationists." At the other extreme were those who taught that essentially all anger was wrong. Fortunately the ventilationists have few advocates today. However, there still remain a number who advocate that anger is essentially wrong, a view held by many Christians today. This view fosters a myriad of problems that will be elaborated on throughout the book.

The knowledge and insights shared in this book come not only out of a sound psychological framework, but I believe are consistent with the Bible, which is a vitally important guideline for myself and for many readers. Therefore, while Christians will find the principles in this book to be consistent with their beliefs, I believe that non-Christians will also find the methods taught for handling anger to be useful, even though they may not agree with me theologically. I have taught the concepts in this book to both secular and religious audiences with equally effective results.

As for my own experience, I grew up with poor modeling of anger. Often I could sense tension in the air at home, and there was seldom constructive communication during conflicts. Occasionally a strong angry remark would be made, followed by a cold war. I knew that what I saw couldn't be the solution to handling anger, and I have since learned and taught what I can about how to constructively handle anger.

The problems and solutions that I discuss in the following pages are those that I have personally dealt with in my own life and have seen in the lives of innumerable patients. This book comes not only out of a theoretical framework, but out of practical experience, both personal and professional. I can gladly say over time, I have seen the solutions prove very effective in people's lives.

All the examples used in this book are real, but names and incidental features have been altered sufficiently to preserve the privacy of the individuals involved.

I greatly appreciate the tremendous assistance in typing and editing by my wife, Betty, and my niece, Lyn Carlson.

—*Dwight L. Carlson*

1

Misconceptions About Anger

Jan is an attractive college sophomore who stood several months ago on top of the Vincent Thomas Bridge in San Pedro, California, and seriously contemplated jumping the equivalent of 18 stories to her death. Several weeks ago she attempted suicide by taking an overdose of pills. She sat in my office, ready for this week's psychotherapy session. She started by telling me about an event that happened Thursday afternoon. Jan said she felt funny and confused, and walked aimlessly around the campus and the adjacent shopping mall. This confusion lasted for several hours, and then she returned to her dorm and felt better. "That was it," she said. "That's all!"

"You mean you had this episode of aimless confusion for several hours and that's what was troubling you?" I asked.

"Yes," she said.

I waited for more, but all I got was silence. I asked about further feelings or anything else that might have happened that day. Still she came up with nothing. She had had no other feelings, and nothing unusual had happened during the 24 hours prior to her episode. Already 20 minutes of the session had passed, and we seemed to be making little progress.

Eventually I asked, "What do you normally do on Thursday afternoon around 2:30?"

She replied that she normally went to her chemistry class.

"So you didn't attend class Thursday?" I questioned.

"No," she answered. When I asked her why, she didn't seem to know.

Because I knew that Jan was very conscientious and that this was highly unusual behavior for her, I questioned her further. Eventually I found out that in the previous chemistry class her lab partner had had trouble understanding the instructions, so Jan tried to help by quietly explaining them. But the instructor heard the whispering and snapped, "Be quiet, Jan." Jan instantly quieted down and didn't say another word the rest of the class.

When I asked her how she felt about the instructor's remark, she at first denied having any reaction or feeling anything. But as I probed further and pointed out that there must have been a powerful reason why she didn't attend class, she finally was able to get in touch with a slight feeling of irritation at her lab partner and her teacher.

You see, one of Jan's basic problems is that she is a very sensitive person who has always been uncomfortable with feelings of anger. When she became a Christian, she was taught that anger is sin. Therefore, she progressively hid from herself her own feelings of irritation and anger. This powerful source of energy had become repressed to such a degree that she literally felt nothing. Even when she was ready to jump off the bridge, she said she felt "numb." When people insulted her she wouldn't feel hurt or angry, but on the other hand, when something good happened, she wasn't able to feel happy either.

Jan illustrates Misconception #1 that many people have about anger: *If you don't look, feel, or seem angry, you don't have an anger problem.*

Joseph Cooke, a missionary to Thailand, exemplifies another misconception people have about anger. In his book *Free for the Taking* he says

> ...squelching our feelings never pays. In fact, it's rather like plugging up a steam vent in a boiler. When the steam is stopped in one place, it will come out somewhere else. Either that or the whole business will blow up in your face. And bottled-up feelings are just the same. If you bite down your anger, for example, it often comes out in another form that is much more difficult to deal with. It changes into sullenness, self-pity, depression, or snide, cutting remarks....
>
> Not only may bottled-up emotions come out sideways in various unpleasant forms; they also may build up pressure until they simply have to burst forth. And when they do, someone is almost bound to get hurt....
>
> I remember that for years and years of my...life, I worked to bring my emotions under control. Over and over again, as they cropped up, I would master

them in my attempt to achieve what looked like a gracious, imperturbable Christian spirit. Eventually, I had nearly everybody fooled, even in a measure my own wife. But it was all a fake. I had a nice-looking outward appearance; but inside, there was almost nothing there....

And way underneath, almost completely beyond the reach of my conscious mind, the mass of feelings lay bottled up. I didn't even know they were there myself, except when their pale ghosts would surface now and then in various kinds of unsanctified attitudes and reactions. But they were there nevertheless. And the time came when the whole works blew up in my face, in an emotional breakdown.

All the things that had been buried so long came out in the open. Frankly, there was no healing, no recovery, no building a new life for me until all those feelings were sorted out, and until I learned to know them for what they were, accept them, and find some way of expressing them honestly and nondestructively.[1]

Despite his best intentions, Joseph Cooke fell victim to Misconception #2: *If you ignore your hurts and anger, they will go away and won't cause you any trouble later on.*

Joe is a 26-year-old machinist. One thing is sure—he doesn't have any trouble expressing his feelings. He makes it quite clear when he is angry—a little too clear. Everyone was quite aware of the fact that he was hostile when he broke his guitar into a thousand pieces just because his friend criticized his playing. His son knew he was angry at him for leaving his bike in the driveway, because Joe deliberately drove over the back wheel of the bike. His wife was very aware of his feelings when he broke windows, doors, dishes, and furniture.

Joe was applying the theory popularized in the 1970s that said that if you just get your feelings and anger out in the open, you'll feel better and everything will be fine. But there's just one problem with this view—it doesn't work, and in the long run, it destroys one's health and relationships. It certainly wasn't working for Joe, who was usually miserable and frequently on the brink of suicide. He had fallen prey to the tempting Misconception #3: *Just let all your feelings and anger hang out—just get them out of your system—and you'll solve your anger problems.*

Brenda, a professional-looking secretary, is very aware of her hurts and angry feelings, but she would never dream of expressing them like Joe does. She tells me, "I can't get angry at anyone—if I could, I wouldn't be here. I can't get angry because then no one would love me." She adds, "I can't even get mad at a guy who tries to seduce me."

Brenda typifies a host of patients I have known who wouldn't hurt anyone, who are never angry, and who seem to have an ideal temperament. Individuals like Brenda are friendly, well-liked, "nice" people. But they pay a tremendous price for their perpetual "niceness." After a few years, physical and emotional illnesses often develop that affect their health, their relations with family members, and their job performance. Brenda is a victim of Misconception #4: *It won't cost me too much emotionally to be a nice person who never gets angry at anybody.*

Mary, a 42-year-old bank teller, sought my help for dizziness and stomach symptoms. Her internist had been unable to find a physical cause for her symptoms, which were so severe that they were interfering with her job. Upon questioning, Mary didn't seem to be harboring any bitterness or anger toward anybody she knew, including her husband of 20 years. But as therapy progressed it became apparent that she had buried a number of hurts over the years. At first she didn't see any correlation between these old hurts and her current symptoms.

Our next obstacle was her failure to realize that a dedicated Christian could not only have such feelings but could resolve them in a constructive way. She was afraid that if she expressed her true feelings to her non-Christian husband, he would think less of her faith, might leave her, or might even have a heart attack and die, leaving her to blame herself. Eventually she started gingerly applying the principles outlined in this book, and to her amazement, her relationship with her husband got better—not worse. A new-found love developed between them, and her symptoms were resolved.

Mary illustrates Misconception #5: *If I express my hurts and anger to the person I'm angry at, our relationship will suffer.*

It is my opinion that at least 50 percent of all emotional, psychosomatic, and interpersonal problems (including familial and marital problems) are the result of poorly handled anger. In addition, it has been repeatedly proven that many physical illnesses—such as hypertension, heart attacks, and even cancer—are more common in individuals who have a problem with anger. What is more staggering is that a large percentage of these people don't even realize that they have an anger problem. Some of them may perhaps be aware that they are nursing a backlog of old hurts, but many others are not aware of the role that feelings and anger play in their lives. As you've been reading about these patients, perhaps you've been saying to yourself, "I'm sure glad I don't have a problem with anger like they do." But, I ask you to consider the fact that it is precisely the person who thinks he never gets angry who often has the most serious problem with anger. He may be chronically late, sulk, whine, or stew; he may be cynical, envious, or catty; he may savor secret injustices, gossip "self-righteously," or engage in hurtful humor; he may be sarcastic, make caustic comments, or develop a martyr complex; but if you ask him if he has a problem with anger, he will smile innocently and say, "Why, no—I never get angry."

The problem is that this person doesn't see these things as symptomatic of an underlying problem with anger. Like many of us, he has a very simplistic notion of what anger is. Most of us think of a person who has a problem with anger as someone who yells at his kids and kicks his dog. But more often it is the person who suffers in stoic silence who has a problem with anger. The people who bury anger or who express it in such camouflaged forms as bitterness, cynicism, or envy often fail to recognize the indicators of anger in their lives. They don't recognize as anger the little inner twinge when a friend makes an ever-so-carefully-phrased insult in the middle of a conversation. They don't recognize as anger the vague bitterness at their family for not appreciating all that they do for them.

Many people who are unable to recognize anger in their lives do sense that they have been hurt many times in the past, and that many of these hurts have not been resolved. If you find that you usually sense hurts rather than feelings of anger, perhaps it would be helpful for you to substitute the word *hurts* with the word *anger* when you read this book so that it is more applicable to you.

The root cause of many of these misconceptions about anger is a distrust and even a denial of our emotions. The fallacy of denying our emotions of hurt and anger can be illustrated by the following example:

My first car was plagued with a multitude of problems, including overheating. In those days the temperature gauge was an actual needle that would slowly rise higher and higher. My anxiety level would have a parallel response, and I'd nervously sweat out the miles to my destination, or at least to the nearest gas station.

I could have saved myself a great deal of anguish by putting my hand over the gauge or even painting it black so I couldn't see the needle rise. I might have saved myself a lot of anxiety. However, if I had done that, then I wouldn't have known the car was overheating until I saw steam pouring out from under the hood, meaning that something was seriously wrong with the car.

Although painting over the temperature gauge may seem like a ridiculous thing to do, it is precisely what many people do with anger. They ignore it and even deny its very existence until it boils over, at which point they can't avoid it any longer. But by that time it may have caused incalculable harm to the person himself and to those around him.

Just like our cars need a temperature gauge and we would never dream of painting over it, so too we need our emotions and must never deny them. Our feelings, including the feeling of anger, are God-given gifts that will serve us well if we are able to be aware of them and act on them appropriately.

Camouflaging Anger

When people aren't aware of their anger, it often becomes camouflaged in a variety of ways. Take the case of Mark. Mark is a church leader who has a big smile on his face as he greets visitors every Sunday. He is very willing to help out those in need. He teaches a Bible study. People talk about how kind and understanding he is—he always has time to listen. But little do they know about what goes on at home. Only Mark's family knows how verbally abusive he can be. For example, this morning as he herded his family into the car, the tension was palpable. The children weren't ready to leave on time, and he went on and on to his wife about how "*she* was responsible." But when he arrived on the church parking lot, a sudden metamorphosis took place. Mark put on his Sunday-go-to-meeting-face and instantly became the model Christian. We might call this behavior *the righteous camouflage.* Unfortunately, as the book *Battered into Submission* accurately portrays, this is a far more common and tragic occurrence than we realize.[2]

Mr. Jones, a 58-year-old executive, sat in my office and told me that he wanted out of his marriage of 32 years. He felt he could cope better with divorce than with this marriage. He described himself as a person who wanted "peace at any price" after yielding for years to the pressures and demands of his wife. He was, as he put it, "always capitulating."

Mr. Jones said that he "faked the harmony" but always resented the deception. He concluded that it would take years to work out the problems in his marriage, and that he didn't have that much time left. For the first 20 years of his married life he hadn't been aware of what was going on. He became conscious of the unhealthy relationship 12 years ago, but hadn't altered his behavior. For the last six months he had been having physical symptoms; however, they disappeared three weeks ago when he told his wife he was leaving.

Mr. Jones illustrates yet another form that camouflaged anger can take—the don't-make-waves, *peace-at-any-price* individual. This individual will take the blame for anything, even things for which he is in no way responsible. He is self-effacing and never appears to be angry. But the peace is a sham. He often has psychosomatic complaints that serve as a means of dissipating the anger. This kind of person is frequently married to someone who is more aggressive, who tyrannizes the peace-at-any-price individual. This person may think he is carrying out the Beatitudes (see Matthew 5:3-12) because he is always turning the other cheek. In reality, it is a poor counterfeit. Sooner or later the results of this kind of behavior will catch up with him.

Another way a person can camouflage his anger is by becoming a *stamp saver*. Back in the 1950s and 1960s many stores gave out S&H Green Stamps and Blue Chip Stamps as a reward for shopping at their stores. When you filled up a book of stamps, you could cash the book in for some merchandise. I call people who store up injustices *stamp savers*. This person is the one who carefully saves up each little grievance, annoyance, or irritation. He tells himself that each aggravation is not enough to deal with in itself. If asked, he would probably deny that there was anything bothering him at all. He may tell himself that the problem is so small that he shouldn't make an issue of it—he should be able to forget it.

But in fact he doesn't forget. He pastes a stamp somewhere in his head. When the book is full, he impulsively cashes it in. The last stamp may have been a very minor incident, but out comes pent-up rage that baffles the recipient and sometimes the stamp saver himself. This outbreak may then be justified by a detailed cataloging of all past offenses.

The fourth form that camouflaged anger can take is the *silent approach*. This person suddenly retreats into an icy silence when something is bothering him. If you ask if anything is wrong, he often flatly denies it, but he usually manages to let everyone know he's upset by making terse or grumpy remarks, or closing the kitchen cupboards just a little bit harder than normal. The people around this silent person often don't know what has upset him, and asking him doesn't help, since he usually won't say anything until he is good and ready to do so.

Some years ago when I was practicing internal medicine, a colleague of mine referred a patient to me. As he was telling me about her physical complaints, he commented, "You know, she's *gooey sweet*—I'm sure she's covering up something, but I haven't figured out what it is yet." As I got to know this woman better, I became convinced that he was right. Her sweetness was saccharin and very tacky. There was something phony about it, something artificial. Often underneath such a gooey-sweet façade is a great deal of anger.

Another camouflage is *criticism*. This angry individual is critical and sometimes sarcastic about everything. In comparison with the previous camouflages, this veneer tends to wear a bit thin. Often his criticisms are supported by seemingly well-founded intellectual or rational reasoning, yet through it all something seems wrong, and you can sense an undertone of anger, hostility, and negativism.

The seventh form that camouflaged anger can take is that of the *passive-aggressive* attitude. This attitude is characterized by aggressive behavior exhibited in passive ways such as obstructionism, pouting, procrastination, intentional inefficiency, or taking the opposite point of view on an issue. The passive-aggressive person tends to be out of sync with others. If you say something is white, he'll call it black; if you say it's black, he'll say it's white. He is often late and keeps others waiting for him. Although he is perpetually pleasant mannered, he still manages to upset other people's plans. For example, let's say you have planned a committee meeting on a certain Thursday night, but when you check it out with Bill, he says, "Oh, I'm so sorry—I have another obligation that night. But I could do it on Wednesday." You go to great lengths to change your own schedule and get everyone to agree to the alternate arrangement. You then call Bill back, only to have him say, "Oh, I'm so very, very sorry, but my Aunt Jenny will be in town that night. However, I could make the meeting if it were Tuesday night." Prolonged contact with this kind of person can be extremely frustrating.

This list of ways to camouflage anger is not all-inclusive; there are as many ways to camouflage anger as there are people to camouflage it. Camouflages are emotional subterfuges we devise for ourselves—subterfuges that extract a tremendous toll on everyone involved.

The Catastrophic Results of Mishandled Anger

Tom is a 54-year-old CPA who does not fit what, in the past, has been called Type A behavior, which is character-ized by an excessive drive, time urgency, competitiveness, and impatience.[3] Tom does not seem to have these traits. Rather, he appears to have a happy home life and is involved in community affairs. However, nine years ago he developed hypertension, and recently, after getting off the phone with an IRS agent, he had severe chest pain. The paramedics were called and he was rushed to the hos-pital. He had a severe heart attack and nearly died.

Everyone who knew Tom was surprised. He had never smoked and there was very little heart disease in his family. If you only knew him casually, you would think he was a very relaxed person, but once you got to know him better, you would discover hostility, frustration, and cyni-cism.

Tom has what are called the "toxic" or "hidden" com-ponents of Type A behavior: anger, hostility, and cyni-cism.[4] Other researchers have found that coronary artery disease is caused or aggravated by anger, hostility, and aggressiveness.[5] The common denominator found in all studies is anger and hostility.[6]

Anger Kills

Tom is one of the at least 36,000 people who have heart attacks each year in the United States that are triggered by anger.[7] It has now been clearly established that anger can precipitate a heart attack[8] and cause a fatal heart rhythm known as *ventricular fibrillation.*[9] Furthermore, anger accelerates coagulation, which in turn increases the likelihood that a blood clot will block a vessel.[10] Hostility has also been shown to raise a person's total cholesterol level and the "bad" LDL cholesterol, while lowering the "good" HDL cholesterol.[11]

Once a person has heart disease, any surge of stress[12] or anger[13] that comes along causes the vessels to constrict more.[14] This is just the opposite of what the heart needs, because the constriction makes it hard for oxygen to get to the heart. A heart with constricted vessels is not able to pump blood as well when the person gets angry.[15] One researcher found that "chronic feelings of anger, hostility, and aggression increase the risk of atherosclerosis and coronary heart disease by as much as *five times over normal.*"[16] So it is not surprising that a person with underlying heart disease will have a much shorter life expectancy unless he learns how to handle his anger more constructively.[17]

But back to Tom, our 54-year-old CPA. How does Tom's high blood pressure fit into the picture? It increases the likelihood of diseased blood vessels developing not only in the heart, but throughout the body. And where does hypertension come from? Well, you guessed it—often it develops as a result of anger, especially in the form of hostility.[18] There is clear evidence that inadequate anger management skills can lead to hypertension.[19] Furthermore, studies show that if Tom had learned anger-coping methods, this might have prevented or decreased his hypertension and possibly his heart attack.[20]

Essentially the same factors that lead to heart attacks result in strokes. With all his hostility, Tom was fortunate that he didn't have a stroke along with his heart attack. In one study, 54 percent of stroke victims said they had been angry right before the stroke.[21] Strokes are caused by plaques, which are abnormal deposits on the inner wall of an artery. There is a significant correlation between the amount of plaque and the amount of poorly-handled anger a person has.[22] Hostility also increases the tendency of blood clots to form around these plaques.[23]

Evidence also suggests that hostile people have weaker immune systems.[24] There is even evidence that hostility is associated with an increased mortality rate, regardless of the cause of death.[25] In other words, whether you die from a disease or from an accident, you are more likely to die at an early age if you don't know how to deal with the anger in your life. In one sobering study, a group of 225 doctors who had a high level of hostility were *seven times* more likely to have died from *any cause* after 25 years, as compared to those with a low level of hostility.[26] Another study concluded that 20 percent of the population has levels of hostility high enough to be dangerous to their health.[27]

The Overtly Angry Person

If anger is so bad, why don't we get rid of it by just letting it out? Why not rant and rave and get it out of our system? Contrary to popular opinion, simply ventilating our anger also carries significant health risks. Most significantly, it causes coronary heart disease, increased blood clot formation, hypertension, and depression.[28] One researcher summarized the problem as follows: "The more the anger, the greater the risk."[29]

Then there is the cost to personal relationships when you have a tirade. Joe, described in chapter 1, comes to mind. What was the cost to Joe for losing his temper all the time? He was chronically unhappy. He frequently entertained thoughts of suicide, and he had ostracized himself from almost all his friends and relatives. Soon after seeing me he lost his job, which created more financial problems. All of this put tremendous pressure on his marriage. It's little wonder that high levels of hostility have been shown to result in more marital conflict and less marital satisfaction.[30]

Thus, expressing his anger—which is commonly referred to in the literature as "anger out"—was not the answer. What Joe needed was to learn how to handle his anger in a constructive way.

Repressing Anger

Many Christians think that all anger is wrong—that it is sin. As a result, they simply try to ignore it, pushing it down when they feel it. Such a response is not helpful, for if they continue doing this, in time they will become totally unaware of their anger.

People vary along a wide spectrum in their awareness of their anger. At one end of the spectrum, both the individual and others may be aware that the person is suppressing his anger. At the other end of the spectrum, the person may actually be convinced that there is no anger in his life. This denial of anger may occur at an unconscious level, making the individual totally unaware that he is repressing negative emotions. He may even try to convince others that he isn't angry. We're all familiar with the person who snaps, "No, I'm not angry!" when quite obviously he is. In some cases, however, the person who protests that he isn't angry is quite calm and collected and actually *feels* no anger. He may have repressed his anger to such a degree that he is completely numb to his feelings, while in reality a great deal of anger is buried deep within him.

Anger, in my opinion, is like energy. It cannot be destroyed, but it can be stored, its form can be changed, or it can be properly discharged. When we bury the anger within us and repeatedly deny its existence, I believe it accumulates in what I call the *unresolved anger fund.*[31] The more we push down anger, the more deposits we make in our unresolved anger fund. This stockpiled anger will then express itself through sundry physical or emotional symptoms. As one researcher put it: "The inhibition or active holding back of thoughts, [and] emotions...can become manifested in disease....we believe that *the failure to confront a trauma* forces the person to live with it in an unresolved manner."[32]

Researchers refer to anger, especially chronic anger and hostility that is turned in upon oneself, as "anger in." To refer to a person as an "anger in" individual is a little clumsy; therefore, I usually refer to this person as a "suppressor" or "the suppressor."

Earlier in this chapter, we reviewed the myriad of illnesses that overt anger causes. However, suppressed anger is just as lethal. One study found that the most severe forms of coronary heart disease are often found in individuals who denied hostility in themselves.[33] Numerous studies have evaluated the relationship between anger and high blood pressure. It is now clear that abnormal expression of anger, whether it is "anger in" or "anger out," causes significant elevation in blood pressure.[34] Those least likely to have elevated blood pressure are those who respond to what could potentially be anger-producing situations with what is called a "reflective response." They problem-solve the situation and handle it appropriately.[35] The bottom line is that inappropriately handled anger—whether "anger in" or "anger out"—contributes to high blood pressure.

"The suppressor" of anger does one or more of the following: 1) he consciously inhibits his anger; 2) he denies that he is feeling angry in situations in which most people would feel anger; 3) he experiences guilt after expressing anger.[36] This person often gives "a more benign appraisal" to conflict situations than is appropriate.[37]

Individuals who suppress anger have been described by researchers as nice, compliant, appeasing, accommodating, and nonassertive. They often are emotionally contained. They chronically block any expression of needs and feelings, especially anger. They avoid conflict, suppressing any reaction that may offend others. They also tend to brood when hurt by others.

The kinds of problems that a suppressor is likely to develop are legion. We have already discussed anger's role in hypertension[38] and coronary artery disease.[39] Anger turned inward can cause depression;[40] however, we now realize that there are many other factors that can lead to depression.[41] And, not many people realize that suppressed anger can increase the incidence of cancer—especially cancer of the large colon and breast cancer.[42]

There is a whole laundry list of other illnesses that have been related to anger. They include psychosomatic illnesses, colitis, eating disorders, digestive problems, TMJ (Temporomandibular Joint Pain), musculoskeletal pain, lower back pain, headaches, hives, asthma, obesity, dermatological conditions, sexual problems, fatigue, sleep disorders, sundry emotional problems, and susceptibility to infections.[43]

People with these kinds of symptoms often feel too uncomfortable or threatened to deal with the underlying feelings. Their unconscious mind tries to do them a favor by bottling up the feelings, only to have them manifest themselves in socially acceptable forms of physical symptoms. This only compounds the problem: Now there is worry about a possible physical illness, while the real problem of anger is left unrecognized as the source of the person's difficulties.

Anger Really Kills

People are like volcanoes. They can lay dormant for long periods, but when there is enough heat and pressure an eruption occurs. This is exactly what happens in many homicides.

It is interesting to note that a *majority* of all homicides occur among family members. That's because home is the place where feelings of anger are most apt to erupt. The most likely victim is usually the person's spouse, lover, or friend, and the most likely place for the homicide to occur is in the person's own home. So, many murderers are, in fact, *not* individuals with past criminal records. One author characterizes these people as having "over-controlled hostility." He describes this person as being mild, passive, and naive, one who keeps his underlying feelings—particularly those of anger—well-controlled and concealed, even from his own awareness. Ultimately his hostile feelings erupt in a homicide.[44]

Once I heard a psychiatrist speak who had examined hundreds of prisoners charged with or convicted of murder. He said that a high percentage of the prisoners hadn't wanted to hurt anyone, and they never seemed to get angry or to have a problem with anger. They were often law-abiding citizens who didn't even have a traffic ticket on their record. What happened? In my opinion, these people didn't know how to recognize and deal constructively with small amounts of anger, and they allowed it to build in their unresolved anger fund. A slight provocation one day was enough to make them explode, and they took out their violent feelings on someone they knew.

The cost of anger is truly staggering. Consider the following statistics alone: The United States has the highest homicide rate of any Western industrialized country;

homicide is the second-leading cause of death among 15-to-24-year-olds; 40 percent of all women murdered in the United States die at the hands of their husbands; and at least two million women are battered by their husbands or intimate acquaintances each year.[45] Add to this the role anger can play in causing heart attacks, strokes, other illnesses, and troubled interpersonal relationships. Indeed, the cost of anger is mind-boggling.

Biblical Principles About Anger

Many of us have been told in church that anger is a sin, with certain Scripture verses quoted during sermons to prove the point. If you look up these verses, indeed they seem to say that anger is wrong. However, in other places you'll find verses that seem to say anger is all right. How do we reconcile this apparent discrepancy?

Among the verses that seem to say that anger is wrong are Ephesians 4:31, which says, "Let all...anger...be put away"; Psalm 37:8, which tells us, "Cease from anger"; and Matthew 5:22 in the Sermon on the Mount, "If you are only angry, even in your own home, you are in danger of judgment!" (TLB).

On the other hand, some verses seem to condone anger. Perhaps the most striking verses to this effect are Psalm 4:4, which reads, "Be angry, and do not sin" (NKJV), and Ephesians 4:26: "Be angry, and yet do not sin."

A careful study of the Bible reveals that most of the important people in it got angry, contrary to the stereotypes we have of them today. Moses was a patriarch who, without question, was blessed of God. However, he sometimes became extremely angry. For example, when he returned from receiving the Ten Commandments and the Law on Mount Sinai, he discovered that in his absence the Israelites had started worshiping idols. He became so enraged that he smashed the stone tablets on which the Law was written (Exodus 32:19). Then there's David, who was a man after God's own heart (Acts 13:22). Yet he became angry at God when a man was killed while trying to protect the ark of God (2 Samuel 6:6-8).

We could cite other verses in which men of God got angry. However, we still might not be able to conclude anything about anger because it could be argued that their expression of anger was sinful. For example, one could argue that while Moses should indeed have reprimanded the Israelites, he should not have let himself get so carried away that he smashed the sacred Law of God. One could also argue that David should not have become angry at God.

Nevertheless, there are two Personages in the Bible whom we cannot accuse of sinning when they got angry. Do you know who, in the Bible, got angry most often? Not the Pharisees, nor the Philistines, nor any other assorted heathen. It was God Himself—God, who is without sin. The Hebrew word for *anger* appears approximately 455 times in the Old Testament, and of these, 375 times it refers to the anger of God.

Jesus also became quite angry at times, contrary to the image we have of Him as a nice, quiet soul. When Jesus was about to heal the man with the paralyzed hand, He got upset at the hardened, calloused hearts of the onlookers around Him. The Bible says He looked "around at them with anger" (Mark 3:5). In Mark 11:15-17 we find Jesus driving out the parasitic money changers in the temple with a whip, shouting after them, "Is it not written, 'My house shall be called a house of prayer for all nations? But you have made it a robbers' den.'" In Matthew 23 He lashes out at the hypocritical Pharisees, calling them "whitewashed tombs...full of dead men's bones"! (verse 27).

Thus, some verses seem to indicate that we shouldn't become angry, while others almost tell us that if we are to follow Christ's and God's examples, there are times when we should get angry. How can we reconcile this apparent contradiction? How can we harmonize one verse in which God Himself is angry with another verse in which God commands us not to be angry?

Biblical Analysis of Anger

One way to shed light on this matter is to study the meanings of the various words for *anger* in the original languages in which the Bible was written. We might find out that there are different words for anger with different shades of meaning. For example, there could be one word for anger that denotes God's justified anger, meaning a sort of detached, righteous indignation, while a different word could be used for Saul's unjustified anger when he tried to kill David, meaning a malicious, vindictive rage (1 Samuel 19:10).

The Hebrew word that is most frequently translated "anger" is *aph*. This word appears several hundred times in the Hebrew Old Testament. It is usually used to describe

God's obviously appropriate anger, such as we see in Numbers 11:1: "Now the people became like those who complain of adversity in the hearing of the LORD; and when the LORD heard it, His anger was kindled, and the fire of the LORD burned among them and consumed some of...the camp." However, this same word *aph* describes Moses' strong but questionable emotions when he smashed the stone tablets against the mountain.

Not only is this word used to describe God's appropriate anger and Moses' questionable anger, but it is also the word used to denote clearly inappropriate anger, like when Balaam beat his donkey (Numbers 22:27). Psalm 37:8 also uses this word: "Cease from anger, and forsake wrath: fret not thyself in any wise to do evil" (KJV). Thus exactly the same word is used to describe appropriate, questionable, and inappropriate anger.

When we turn to the New Testament, which was written in Greek, one of the more common words that is translated "anger" is *orge*. While the word originally referred to any natural impulse, desire, or disposition, it later came to signify anger. It was thought of as an internal motion, like the juices in plants or fruit, and meant the natural disposition, temper, character, or impulse of a thing. As in the Old Testament, this word is sometimes used to describe appropriate anger, such as God's or Christ's anger (Mark 3:5; Romans 9:22; Hebrews 3:11). Yet it is the same word that is translated "anger" in Ephesians 4:31: "Let all bitterness and wrath and *anger* and clamor and slander *be put away from you*, along with all malice" (emphasis added). The same word is used in James 1:19: "Let everyone be quick to hear, slow to speak and slow to *anger*" (emphasis added). Thus the same word is used to describe both appropriate and inappropriate anger. Another Greek word, *orgizo*, means "to be angry." It is the word used in Matthew 5:22: "I say unto you, that whosoever is angry with his brother without a cause shall be in danger of the judgment" (KJV). This is an extremely strong injunction against this kind of anger. Yet it is exactly the same word that is used in a very positive sense in Ephesians 4:26: "Be angry, and yet do not sin."

I believe that the logical conclusion we can draw is that each of the words translated "anger" is used in neutral, negative, or positive ways, and that we must look at the context of each verse to see whether the anger is justified or not.

Likewise, in our own lives, we must look at the context of each situation to judge whether our anger is justified or not. The conclusion I have come to after years of study and working with patients is that anger *is in and of itself neutral.* It is neither right nor wrong, appropriate nor inappropriate, holy nor sinful.

It is what the anger is based on and how the anger is expressed that determines whether the anger is right or wrong. This parallels perfectly the usual psychological view of anger, which says that anger is an emotion that is, in itself, neutral. It may be appropriate or inappropriate; it may be used constructively or destructively.

Ten Biblical Principles About Anger

The Scriptures offer many guidelines for handling anger properly. Upon reading God's Word carefully, ten important principles become evident:

First, *anger is a communicable attribute of God:* A communicable attribute of God is a quality originating in God that has been transmitted to humans. Therefore, feelings, including anger, are God-given gifts. Genesis 1:26,27 says that God, in His wisdom, created us in His own image, and it is my belief that one of the things He created us with was the ability to get angry. Feelings can be used to help us and to serve God well. To deny feelings is to deny a part of the person God created us to be.

Second, *anger in and of itself is a neutral feeling:* As we have discussed, anger is inherently neither good nor bad, right nor wrong. James reminds his readers in James 5:17 that godly men of old like Elijah were human beings with feelings like ours, something we are prone to forget. Anger can be likened to power, sex, or fire: They are inherently neither right nor wrong in themselves, but rather, the rightness or wrongness is in how they are used. Christians today are trying to make anger wrong, just like earlier generations tried to make virtually all sex wrong, with disastrous results.

Third, *listen to your feelings, but never allow them to control you:* James 1:19 says, "Let everyone be quick to hear, slow to speak and slow to anger." We are told in Proverbs 16:32, "He who is slow to anger is better than the mighty, and he who rules his spirit, than he who captures a city." Proverbs 19:11 adds, "A man's discretion makes him slow to anger." Thus we should be sensitive to our feelings, but never controlled by them. We should never be compelled to act on the basis of our feelings alone.

Fourth, *don't be hasty in expressing your anger:* Ecclesiastes 7:9 says, "Be not hasty in thy spirit to be angry"

(KJV). James 1:19 tells us that we should be slow to take offense or get angry. Proverbs 25:8 says, "Do not go out hastily to argue your case." (See also Nehemiah 9:17, Psalm 103:8; 145:8; Proverbs 15:18; Titus 1:7.)

Fifth, *don't procrastinate in dealing with your anger:* Just as we should not be in a hurry to express our anger, we must also not go to the opposite extreme and delay dealing with it. This is an extremely important point. If another person makes you feel hurt or angry and you know that you need to talk to him about it, you should try to take action in a matter of seconds or minutes, or at the most, a few hours. Many people wait days, weeks, months, or even years. *The emotional weight that untold millions of people carry simply because they have procrastinated in dealing with their hurts and anger would stagger your mind.*

Ephesians 4:26 is applicable here: "Be angry, and yet do not sin; do not let the sun go down on your anger." To not let the sun go down on your anger could be interpreted three different ways:

First of all, the usual interpretation is that it is referring to *time*—that is, that we should resolve the anger before going to sleep at night.

Second, the Greek word *helios,* which is translated "the sun," can also mean "the natural benefits of light and heat…and judgment."[46] Thus an alternate rendering might be, "Don't wait so long in dealing with the anger that the intensity of the *feeling* decreases and sets within you before you take appropriate action." I believe it is useful to deal with the issue while you still feel angry, as long as certain stipulations are met—which will be discussed in detail later.

Finally, several verses in the Bible refer to the day as the time of *opportunity* (see John 9:4 and Galatians 6:10). A third possible interpretation, then, is to deal with our feelings while there is still an opportunity. It is possible that if Christ had waited one day or several days before kicking out the money changers, they might have already been gone and the opportunity lost.

In summary, an interpretation of Ephesians 4:26 might read, "It's appropriate and necessary to be angry, but be very careful that you don't sin in the process. Dissipate the anger constructively before the heat of the emotion is lost, before too much time passes, and before the best opportunity is gone."

Sixth, *when you are angry, you are much more vulnerable to sin:* Note that right after we are told, "Be angry, and yet do not sin; do not let the sun go down on your anger," Paul adds, "And do not give the devil an opportunity" (Ephesians 4:26,27). An example of this is illustrated in Numbers 20:7-11. Moses was angry at the Israelites, and God gave him instructions on how to deal with the problem. Moses disobeyed the instructions—probably because he was so angry he didn't listen carefully to what God was saying. Similarly, our anger can drown out what God is telling us and can "give the devil an opportunity." Proverbs 29:22 warns, "An angry man stirs up strife, and a hot-tempered man abounds in transgression." Proverbs 14:29 tells us, "A wise man controls his temper. He knows that anger causes mistakes" (TLB).

Seventh, *anger may be wrong because it is due to sin:* Without a doubt, there are times when anger is wrong because it is inappropriately based. In 2 Chronicles 16:7-10, Asa put his trust in the king of Syria instead of in God. A prophet then told him that his country would have wars because of his sin. Asa became angry, put the prophet in jail, and oppressed his people. He became angry because he didn't like what he heard even though it was the truth, and so he took out his anger on others. In 1 Kings 20 and 21, King Ahab became angry and resentful because he didn't get his own way. Obviously, both of these men's anger was far from righteous. If we have expectations that are inappropriate or sinful and we become angry because we don't get our way, we are sinning in our anger.

Eighth, *if you are chronically angry you are probably sinning:* Another version of Ephesians 4:26 focuses on the danger of nursing our anger and letting it turn into bitterness and resentment: "If you are angry, do not let anger lead you into sin; do not let sunset find you still nursing it; leave no loop-hole for the devil" (NEB). The Scriptures teach that persistent anger that makes us bitter and resentful is sin. Hebrews 12:15 says, "See to it…that no root of bitterness springing up causes trouble, and by it many be defiled."

We sometimes mechanically repeat the part of the Lord's Prayer that says, "Forgive us our debts, as we also have forgiven our debtors," but very few of us stop to consider the consequences of what we are saying. The Amplified Bible's rendering of the verse immediately following the Lord's Prayer says, "But if you do not forgive others their trespasses [their reckless and willful sins, leaving them, letting them go, and giving up resentment] neither will your Father forgive you your trespasses" (Matthew 6:15). Thus, clinging stubbornly to resentment is very destructive to us because it blocks God's forgiveness.

Ninth, *vindictive anger is wrong:* The Scriptures clearly teach that vindictive, malicious anger is wrong. Almost every time the phrase "cease from anger" is found in the Bible, it is in the context of vindictive anger. For example, Psalm 37:8 says, "Cease from anger, and forsake wrath." Romans 12:18-21 says, "If possible, so far as it depends on you, be at peace with all men. Never take your own revenge, beloved, but leave room for the wrath of God, for it is written, 'Vengeance is Mine, I will repay', says the Lord. But if your enemy is hungry, feed him, and if he is thirsty, give him a drink; for in so doing you will heap burning coals upon his head. Do not be overcome by evil, but overcome evil with good."

Tenth, *anger may be righteous and its absence may displease God:* The final principle—and perhaps the most startling one—is that in some cases anger may be righteous and its absence may displease God. In other words, we may be sinning by not getting angry. First Samuel 11:6 is a rather remarkable verse: "Then *the Spirit of God* came upon Saul mightily when he heard these words, *and he became very angry*" (emphasis added). The passage goes on to indicate that Saul's anger and the resulting action he took was righteous. In Nehemiah 5:6-9, a prophet, speaking as God's messenger, became angry at the people of Israel as he reprimanded them for their sin. God even commanded Moses to be angry and kill the Midianites in Numbers 25:16,17.

It is no wonder that one commentator writes, "The words 'be ye angry' in Ephesians 4:26 are a present imperative in the Greek text, commanding a continuous action."[47] This verse can be viewed as a command to be angry under certain conditions.

Have you ever considered the possibility that Christ might have sinned if He hadn't gotten angry at the money changers in the temple? There are other examples in the Scriptures of people who probably were sinning because they didn't get angry enough to take corrective action. For example, Eli the priest was warned by God because he didn't rebuke his sons for their sin of desecrating sacrifices to God. Eli, however, was passive. Even when God told Eli that He would kill Eli's entire household, including Eli, all he said was, "Let Him do what seems good" (see 1 Samuel 2:22-4:18). This is in distinct contrast to what most prophets did when they heard God's judgment— they got upset enough to forcefully warn people to turn from their wicked ways, often with positive results, so that God wouldn't punish them.

When the Israelites wanted Aaron to make a golden calf for them to worship, he was passive and gave in to their request. Exodus 32:25 says, "The people were out of control—for Aaron had let them get out of control." Aaron might have been better off if he had had some of Moses' tablet-smashing anger! The church leaders at Corinth undoubtedly would not have received such a strong rebuke from Paul if they had stirred up enough anger to take appropriate action against the incestuous church member (see 1 Corinthians 5).

Another rendering of "Be angry, and yet do not sin" might be, "Be appropriately angry and thereby do not sin." Many people don't get angry when they should, and therefore do not mobilize the energy necessary to deal with some crucially important issues of life. But how is this properly done? We will find out in the upcoming chapters.

How Do You Handle Your Anger?

Anger is defined as an unpleasant emotional state of varying intensity from mild irritation to rage. It is a feeling of displeasure as a result of a real or imagined threat, insult, put-down, frustration, or injustice to you or to others who are important to you.

Anger has both a cognitive and an emotional component. The cognitive component is the result of a split-second assessment of the perceived mistreatment. The emotional component is the body's automatic emotional response to the recognized provocation.

If the feeling of displeasure is strong, it activates the "fight-or-flight" mechanism in the body, which prepares it for battle or escape. This mechanism releases adrenaline, which, in turn, increases the blood pressure, pulse, and respiratory rate. The person may perspire or feel edgy from the surge of energy that has literally infused the entire body. These intense feelings of displeasure are what most people associate with being angry.

While the layman tends to lump together the terms *anger, hostility,* and *aggressiveness,* researchers have found it useful to have more precise definitions:[48]

• *Anger* is defined as a transitory emotion or *feeling* of displeasure.[49]

• *Hostility* is defined as an *attitude* of ill will or the wish to inflict harm. It is a longer-lasting trait. Hostile sentiments include animosity, resentment, and other chronic forms of anger.[50] It's what I referred to as chronic anger or the "root of bitterness" in the previous chapter. Hostility, when acted on, results in aggressive behavior.

• The term *aggressiveness* refers to punitive or destructive *behaviors* directed toward other individuals or objects. Aggression is an overt act that seeks to attack, destroy, or be hurtful. The Scriptures refer to this as "vengeance."

Anger can further be divided into the categories "anger in" and "anger out." "Anger in" is marked by feelings of anger, hostility, and, in rare instances, aggressiveness that the person turns inward upon himself, whom I am referring to as "the suppressor." The vast majority of individuals are prone to be anger suppressors.[51]

"Anger out" is marked by angry feelings, hostility, or aggressiveness that are expressed externally. Only about 10 percent of the population falls into the "anger out" category. I will sometimes refer to this person as "the aggressor."

Obvious and Hidden Anger

Anger can manifest itself in basically four ways: It can be *known* to the person and to others, it can be *hidden* to others, the person who is angry can be *blind* to it, or it can be *unknown* to both others and the person himself.

These manifestations can be illustrated by a large square divided into four smaller squares (see Illustration 1).[52] The upper two squares, which are shaded, represent the anger that the person himself is aware of. The two squares on the left side with hatch marks represent the anger in the person that the world at large is aware of.

1. The upper left square represents an individual whose feelings are known by both the world at large as well as by

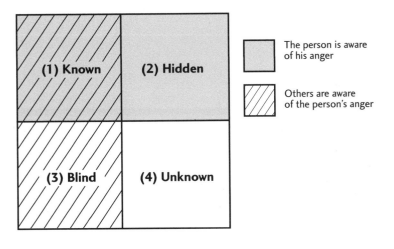

The person is aware of his anger

Others are aware of the person's anger

The Visibility of Anger
Illustration 1

the person himself. We may say that this person's angry feelings are *known*.

2. In the square in the upper right-hand corner, the person himself is aware of the anger, but the world isn't; thus, this person's anger is *hidden*. At times this may be very appropriate. For example, when a person is cut off by another driver on the freeway, he may feel a surge of rage, but in my opinion, it is prudent in this day and age that he not express that anger. It is better to choose to pass over the issue (which we will discuss later in the book). However, if a person chronically uses this method for handling anger, he will become a suppressor.

3. In the lower left-hand square of our illustration, the person himself is unaware of his anger, but the world at large is aware of it. The person is *blind* to his own anger. This is never healthy for the individual. Others see this person as angry, upset, or difficult to get along with, but the person himself is unaware that anger is his basic problem.

4. Last of all, and most serious of all, is the person whose anger has been denied and repressed to such an extent that neither the person himself nor the world around him is aware that anger is buried within him. The person whose feelings are *unknown* is depicted by the lower right-hand square. This individual often has difficulty being in touch with any of his feelings, including joy or happiness. He may have a myriad of symptoms. He could appear cold, aloof, or even overly nice, but neither he nor the world around him is aware of the important role of anger in the development of his problems.

Obviously, this chart is oversimplified—people cannot be categorized so neatly into four little squares. Furthermore, we all probably operate, at one time or another, in different ones of these squares. There are three important lessons that we can learn from this diagram. One point is that other people may be aware of a person's anger while the person himself may not be. Thus it is often crucial that the person remain open to the input of others when trying to understand himself.

Second, both the person himself and others may be totally unaware that anger is the root problem, and thus the person can spend untold hours and dollars trying to find other causes for the physical and emotional symptoms. If the person fails to recognize the fact that hurts and anger can be the cause of a host of seemingly unrelated physical and emotional problems, he won't get very far in treating his problem.

Third, we should strive to be operating in the *known* and *hidden* spheres; dealing with our angry feelings quickly and constructively, so that they can assist us in healthy living as God intended.

Levels of Maturity in Handling Anger

For years I have heard suggestions for dealing with anger like "Slam the door, it will do you good." Many times I have wrestled with these ideas. Do I agree with them? Is it good to slam a door? I came to the conclusion that slamming a door may be a positive step for someone who is not in touch with his anger or who always buries it. On the other hand, some people who slam doors also break furniture. For them, slamming doors isn't beneficial unless it is a less destructive act than they might otherwise have performed. On yet another hand, a more mature individual may actually be regressing if he slams a door.

The thing to realize is that we don't handle anger maturely or immaturely, with no stages in-between. Rather, there are various levels of maturity in which we deal with our anger. The method of treatment will then vary according to how maturely the person handles his anger, just as a medical prescription varies according to the specific illness and how sick a patient is. We must resist the temptation to give a person blanket solutions to their anger problem. We cannot tell everybody that the way to handle their anger is to slam the door. For those who have already broken every door and window in the house, this would obviously not be advisable.

The diagram "Visibility and Maturity of Handling Anger" clarifies the different levels of maturity (see Illustration 2). The vertical axis represents how maturely a person handles his anger—the higher up you go on the graph, the more mature the person is. A maturity level of 1 indicates a *very immature* person, while a maturity level of 10 indicates a *very mature* person.

The horizontal axis represents how visible the anger is. The farther you go to the right of the graph, the more visible the person's anger. A person whose anger is largely *hidden* is at "a," while a person whose anger is obvious is at "d."

The shaded area represents that which is within the realm of possibility. For example, the point 10-d represents a person who is both very mature (10) and overtly chron-

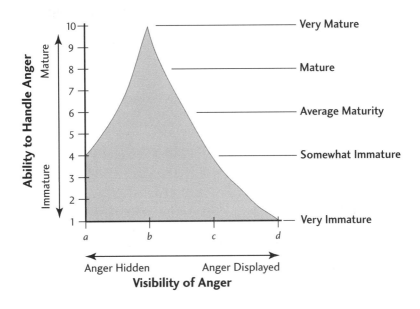

Visibility and Maturity of Handling Anger
Illustration 2

ically angry (d). It is impossible for a person to be both very mature and have a chronic temper, so the point 10-d is not part of the shaded area. Likewise, a person cannot always be calm, cool, and collected—the stereotypical "always nice" person—and be very mature. This person evidently is burying some of his anger, because some conflict in life is inevitable. Thus, I do not show a point 10-a as a possibility. I believe that if a person takes a stand on righteous principles (to be discussed later in this book), he will face conflicts that he will have to directly confront. Even the most mature individual will occasionally display some anger, so I have placed him at point 10-b.

If we look at the bottom of the graph, we see that the *very immature* person is illustrated at maturity level 1. It is apparent from looking at the shaded area that he may, at one extreme, hide his anger and be at point 1-a, or else at the other extreme overtly and frequently display his anger and thus be at point 1-d. It doesn't matter where this person falls on the line between points 1-a and 1-d; he is still at the same degree of immaturity. The only difference is how apparent the person's immaturity is to those observing this individual. The 1-d person will appear to be hostile and even aggressive—the stereotypical "immature" person. On the other hand, the 1-a person may appear on the surface to handle his hostility maturely because he is calm and unemotional in time of stress. But in reality he is as immature as the hostile 1-d person.

Let's look a little closer at some of the possible positions on the graph. At maturity level 10 *(very mature)*, the individual is fully aware of what is going on in a conflict situation. He is aware of his own feelings, including feelings of hurt and anger. He has no residual anger in his unresolved anger fund. He is in full control of his actions—his responses are by choice rather than by reaction. He chooses the best means to handle anger, which will be described later in the book. Only Christ would qualify for this category.

As we move further down the graph we come to the *mature* individual, who I have placed at level 8. He knows his feelings and what causes them, and typically handles them well. This is probably the most mature person you will ever know. Many annoyances that bother other people really won't bother this person. However, when something really does disturb him, this person can be counted on to confront the situation squarely. He will rarely avoid a problem merely because it is uncomfortable to deal with.

Moving down to maturity level 6, the *average maturity* level, we discover someone who usually handles the hurts in his life well. As indicated on the diagram, this person may tend to hide his feelings more and thus may be at 6-a, or he may be more overt in expressing his feelings and be at 6-c.

As we move further down the graph, we find the individual having progressively more difficulty knowing his feelings and handling them well. More physical and emotional problems are appearing, and more unresolved anger is left over from past conflicts. The further down we go, the more we see that people with the same level of maturity can differ markedly in their expression of anger. That is from a to c for the *somewhat immature* and a to d for the *very immature.*

Finally by the time we are to the *very immature,* or level 1, we find an individual who has great difficulty in handling most conflict situations. Often numerous emotional and physical problems are present. Hopelessness and thoughts of suicide become a significant risk. There are tremendous amounts of hurt or anger buried away, of which the person may have little comprehension. At this level we have the potential for extremes in manifestation. At one end is the individual who fits into position 1-a. His anger is hidden from outside observers, or maybe even unknown to himself. Jan, in chapter 1, who was "numb," fits into this category. It is virtually impossible for this person to avoid creating a great deal of problems for others as well as for himself.

At the other extreme is 1-d. This individual is extremely hostile and aggressive to those who get in his way. His anger is readily apparent to others, although the person himself may have little awareness of the extent of his anger. He causes others much distress and, before long, is a very unhappy person himself.

Recently we have seen an increase in road rage, homicides, and mass murders—whether at home, school, work, church, and even at random. It is of interest that a person who is anywhere in level 1 is capable of this behavior. At one extreme is the quiet, often "nice" person who has buried his anger until it becomes so great that it explodes like a volcano. At the other extreme is the person whose anger is apparent to all who know him. The day may come when he bursts forth with a hail of bullets hitting anyone who is in his way.

The purpose of this graph is to help you pinpoint just how maturely you handle anger.

I encourage you to take a moment to consider where you fit into this scheme. Think of various conflict situations you have experienced in the past—a snub from a friend, an irritation at the office, a terse conversation at home—and analyze the maturity of your responses. Consider things such as whether you use any camouflages, whether you try to avoid conflicts, whether you snap at trivial details, whether your anger is visible to those who know you, and whether you take out your frustrations on others.

Preparing to Handle Anger

Recently I saw a 31-year-old man who had buried his hurts and anger for many years, and in the last two years had developed physical symptoms. Only in the couple of months prior to his visit had he been aware of, or at least willing to admit, the emotional basis. He told me, "I just want it [the problem] to go away. I don't want any hassles." For 20 minutes we talked about his suicidal wishes. He just wanted to die or to get into a bad car accident; but, not wanting to hurt others, he rejected these ideas. At the end of the appointment he told me that he didn't want to talk about his problems anymore—even that was too much of a hassle. So he left, not planning to see me again, refusing any referrals or any of the other options offered to him. My heart was very heavy as I watched him leave my office because I knew he was again taking the easy way out, with the strong possibility of suicide as a consequence.

Realize that Conflict Is Normal and Inevitable

Part of this man's problem was that he was unwilling to accept the inevitability of conflict in his life. He just wanted the problem to go away. He didn't want any hassles. Many of us, whether we realize it or not, have the same attitude. Many people who come to see me professionally dislike emotional conflict intensely and will go to great lengths to avoid it. They often make remarks such as, "I don't like conflict" or, "I hate to argue" or, "I can't stand to be around people when they are angry at each other." Although none of these people have actually said they want a conflict-free environment, this is what they are implying.

The only way that such psychological bliss might be achieved would be by going to a deserted island. On the island, one would have to be careful not to communicate with anyone—either by telephone, e-mail, or letter. No one could be allowed to come ashore because then some conflict would eventually develop. Even then, it is doubtful whether a person would be totally free of conflict, because there would be the stress caused by insects, shark-infested waters, and passing hurricanes.

But as we all know, no man is an island. Rather, we are inextricably woven to each other by complex interpersonal relationships.

It is critical to grasp that anger is both normal and inevitable. Most of us agree intellectually that being irritated or upset is a normal part of everyday existence, but emotionally we often don't accept this. We tend to look upon anger as an abnormal state or as a sign of a deficiency in ourselves. We feel vaguely guilty for getting angry at someone, we try not to think about it, or we wish the problem would just go away so we could get back to everyday life.

Realize that Conflict Begins at Home

It is simply a fact of life that the people who are the closest to you are the people with whom you are most likely to get angry. These are the people you have the most interaction with and of whom you have the highest expectations. As a result, they are the people with whom you have the greatest possibility of being angry.

Conflict is normal with those we love most. Having perfect, Christlike love for someone doesn't mean that his or her snoring doesn't bother you. It's true that newlyweds in a state of matrimonial bliss can often ignore little things that normally would irritate them. But this should be regarded as an emotional phase—certainly a desirable one, but an unrealistic standard for everyday living. Just because you feel angry sometimes at your spouse doesn't mean you don't love him or her.

One author concluded that poorly handled anger is the one key issue that explains why so many marriages, which begin with such high hopes, falter and fail. When couples failed to deal effectively with anger, the result was *too many* or *too few* disagreements, which, in turn, destroyed intimacy.[53]

A study showed that a loved one is the target of people's anger 29 percent of the time, 24 percent of the time the anger is directed towards someone well-known and liked, 25 percent of the time it's shown towards an acquaintance, 8 percent of the time towards someone well-known but disliked, and only 8 percent of the time towards someone unknown.[54]

Realize that Confrontation Is Necessary

Bringing conflict out into the open and dealing with it constructively is called *confrontation*. This is something that many people avoid at all costs—and the costs are high.

I'm reminded of a 14-year-old boy whose parents allowed him to control them to such a degree that they would do almost anything he requested. Occasionally he had to get fairly angry before they would cater to his wishes, but most of the time they yielded without much resistance. They came to me for help but would allow the boy to stop treatment whenever he wanted. The boy literally had his parents moving from one state to another because he felt he would be happier in another location. I remember the day I requested that he have a blood test to be sure there was no endocrine disease causing his emotional difficulty. This is a virtually painless test that lasts all of 30 seconds. Before an hour had passed, I had received a phone call from both parents. The boy had created such a fuss over the blood test that the father had been called home from work.

To this day the situation remains unchanged. The boy has never submitted to the blood test. Unfortunately, the price being paid by the parents and the boy is tremendous. He is having extreme difficulty in school; and unless there is a drastic change soon, this controlling behavior will characterize his adult life. But because his parents are afraid of confrontation, they are continuing to yield to his destructive demands. The root of their problem is their fear of confrontation.

Confronting another person should not be construed as a sign of hostility; rather, it indicates that you care enough about the person to work out the problems in the relationship—no matter how painful the process may be. When you express your feelings honestly, it means that you respect and value yourself and the other person. Expressing your deepest feelings can in fact be a very cleansing experience, one in which the love and respect shared between the two people is strengthened. In addition, the other person will think more highly of you, and your own sense of appropriate worth will increase.

Realize Why We Don't Confront

One of my patients was a successful, middle-aged businesswoman who was seriously considering killing herself rather than dealing with a moderate degree of emotional conflict. She was thinking about jumping off a pier to avoid confronting her husband about a problem in raising their teenage son. Like the parents of the 14-year-old boy, she had a paralyzing fear of confrontation.

Many people say that the idea of dealing with their own feelings or someone else's in a constructive, direct fashion is extremely uncomfortable to them. They protest that they "can't stand an argument" and will do anything to avoid it. I'm not, of course, recommending an argument, but an honest sharing of feelings.

So why is confrontation so difficult for many people? Why do some avoid it like the plague? Studies have shown that four main themes appear when people are

asked why they are reluctant to express feelings of anger.[55]
They are:

- Fear of retaliation—that if they confront the other person, he will get back at them or in some way retaliate.

- Fear of rejection—that the other person will no longer want to associate with them.

- Fear of hurting others—that the other person will not be able to handle it if feelings and concerns are honestly shared with him or her.

- A sense of futility—that is, a feeling that confrontation "won't change anything anyway." Many of these people tried to express their needs as children but in response they were emotionally abused. As a result, they have permanently given up trying to share their feelings honestly.

I would like to add to this list some additional reasons I believe keep people from confronting:

- Dealing with anger constructively is often more uncomfortable at first than dealing with it destructively. For "the suppressor," this means doing nothing, which is certainly the easy alternative. It takes time and effort to deal with anger in a positive way, especially when you are first learning how.

- Some people get so much praise for being such a "nice" person that they really don't want to lose that image, and therefore avoid confrontation.

- Many people have been taught that standing up to others is wrong. They have gotten the impression that nice, religious people always accept things meekly.

• Some have only seen confrontation carried out in an aggressive, hostile manner, so they shun all confrontation, associating it with aggressiveness.

• Some people just don't know how to confront. They have never been taught how to handle anger properly and haven't had a model from whom to learn.

• Individuals with a large unresolved anger fund find it very difficult to learn how to handle their anger calmly because they are perpetually hovering near the boiling point. They are fearful of exploding if they try to confront someone.

• Some don't fully grasp the long-term consequences of failing to confront, so they continue on in their old ways.

• There are people who avoid confronting because they think expressing honest feelings will hurt the relationship. But just the opposite is true. If you don't admit being hurt or angry and express it in constructive ways, you may eventually destroy the relationship and ultimately hurt the other person far more extensively.

It is a fact that people can handle constructively expressed hurt or anger much better than repressed or camouflaged anger. Failing to deal constructively with anger may, in the long run, destroy the love that was once there, because if you repress your feelings of anger, you will inevitably squelch all feelings—especially feelings of love. I might add that if you find yourself incapable of feeling love, it may well be because you have a large unresolved anger fund that has not been dealt with.

On the other hand, when you express your honest feelings in constructive ways, true love is never killed, but strengthened. Expressing anger constructively will never damage a worthwhile relationship. If a relationship is destroyed by sharing feelings, it was probably an unhealthy relationship to start with.

Recognize Patterns of Relating

Whether you are in a relationship with a colleague at work or your spouse at home, some typical patterns of relating quickly develop.

The ideal relationship is when two people deal with conflicts honestly and openly. Each person is able to share his feelings without fear. Neither person chronically suppresses anger, but deals with it appropriately and when indicated—openly. This relationship has the least amount of conflict in the long run. This is shown in Illustration 3.

On some occasions I have seen two people who both communicate in what seems to me a very strong, forceful, almost aggressive manner. However, when you ask them about their communication style and if they are able to express their feelings without the other person being hurt, they both answer yes. I therefore have to accept this as a healthy way of relating even though I personally feel uncomfortable with this style. I show this in Illustration 4.

However, it's crucial that a person who comes across very strong be careful when he interacts with a more sensitive person, or he may well become the aggressor. In this

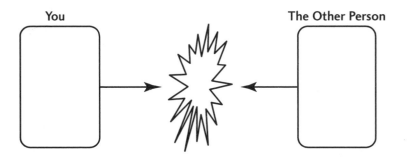

- All conflict is in the open
- Neither person buries anger
- This method results in the least total conflict

The Healthy Relationship
Illustration 3

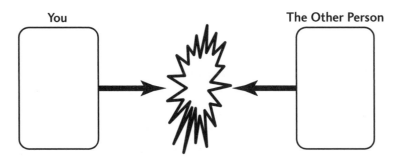

- These individuals communicate strongly
- They have no buried hurt or anger

Two Very Verbal Individuals
Illustration 4

common scenario, we have one person who strongly or aggressively expresses himself, and another person who rarely, if ever, expresses his own feelings, or for that matter, his legitimate needs. In other words, one friend or spouse rides roughshod over the other. The sensitive person can squelch his feelings for a while, but eventually these legitimate needs will cry out for expression. Eventually communication will start to break down, sometimes to the point where the two people have only the most superficial of conversations. The more passive person will stop sharing his feelings and insecurities because he has been hurt so much, and will end up losing his sense of trust in the other person.[56] Meanwhile, the aggressive person may be totally unaware of the fact that he is hurting the other person so much. Eventually the suppressor can be so demoralized that severe physical or emotional symptoms may occur. Ultimately the suppressor may withdraw from the relationship, or lash out in some destructive way. This is shown in Illustration 5.

Illustration 6 represents two individuals who totally dislike conflict. Both are ultra-sensitive to conflict and shun it at all costs. Couples in this category don't share their feelings adequately and, before long, monumental new conflicts can arise within each of them. As suppressors, they can both develop any of the adverse consequences described earlier in this book.

In retrospect, the important thing to note is that the least amount of conflict feasible for a relationship is shown in Illustration 3. In this relationship, the conflict is clearly delineated between the two people and is resolved in constructive ways. *Most notably, neither person is aggressive, nor harbors anger within himself.* This method of handling conflict yields the least amount of overall conflict, emotional stress, and illness.

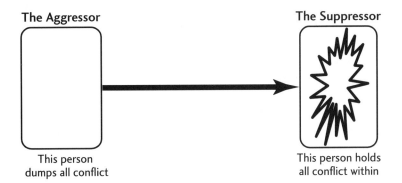

The Aggressor

This person
dumps all conflict

The Suppressor

This person holds
all conflict within

The Aggressive Person and the Suppressor
Illustration 5

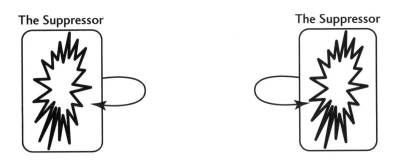

The Suppressor

The Suppressor

- Conflict resides within each person
- There is no external conflict, but tremendous
  amounts of hurt are building up within both individuals

Two People Who Chronically Suppress Their Anger
Illustration 6

Realize the High Cost of Delay

The choice we have in life is not "Do you want conflict or don't you want it?" Rather it is this: "Where, when, and how much conflict do you want?" Do you want to avoid it now and pay a high price later? It's like making a purchase in a department store. At some point you are going to have to pay for it. But do you want to pay for it now, or do you want to charge it and pay for it later with the added cost of compound interest? And in this case, the interest is high.

Avoiding conflict can be likened to refusing a painful injection of penicillin, preferring to suffer with pneumonia instead. Unfortunately, there are many people walking around with emotional pneumonia, so to speak—people who prefer to endure the illness rather than take the necessary cure because it hurts, even if only for a moment.

Can you imagine the amount of hurt, buried anger, and troubled relationships that can build in a person's lifetime if he repeatedly handles anger-producing situations destructively? I see people like that professionally, and it is no small feat to reverse this pattern.

As you start to face the anger problem in your life, things at first may seem to get worse before they get better. I wish I could tell you otherwise; I wish I could offer you an instant-success formula, but I wouldn't be honest if I did. But if you apply the principles described in the upcoming chapters, your rewards will be sizeable. If you are the type of person who is overtly angry, you will have to learn to control yourself in order to confront the person constructively. You may also have to give up some power and control. You may have to give up that momentary twinge of pleasure that comes from getting back at someone who has hurt you.

If you are the type of person who avoids confrontations, you will have to fight your tendency to minimize your feelings instead of dealing with them. You'll also have to learn how to deal with other people's feelings, rather than shy away from them.

Realizing that Anger Can Be Positive

Because anger makes us so uncomfortable, we tend to view it as a negative thing. In reality it can be a very positive agent for change.

One of my patients had had many psychiatric hospitalizations, and one of the contributing factors to her problem was a fully grown son who had been freeloading off of her for years. She seemed unable to confront him about his behavior. Once when her son was going to drive her to the psychiatric hospital, he seemed very pleased at the prospect of getting rid of her. This made her so furious that she marched back into the house with her suitcases and told her son to get out of the house and support himself. This may not have been the most mature way to handle the problem, but for her it was progress, and it is a graphic example of how emotional energy can be used in positive ways.

No wonder it's said that anger can be energizing and has the potential of improving interpersonal relationships and changing behavior.[57] It can have positive effects on both the person who is angry and those who are the target of their anger. It can increase people's understanding and prompt positive change.[58] The Chinese capture this principle in their word for anger, which can be translated as "produces one's energy."[59]

Many constructive movements have been started as a result of someone's anger. When Candy Leightner's child was killed by a drunk driver, she first grieved and then became angry. The anger resulted in her founding Mothers Against Drunk Driving (MADD), which has effectively reduced alcohol-related deaths in the United States. After James Brady, Ronald Reagan's press secretary, was paralyzed by an assassin's bullet, his wife became involved in lobbying efforts to get Congress to restrict the sales of handguns.[60] In previous chapters we have discussed the usefulness of Christ's anger, and the fact that Eli, Aaron, and the church at Corinth would have been well served if they had exhibited some energizing anger.

Anger is like a fire in a fireplace in a remote cabin during a blizzard. If the fire gets out of control it will destroy the occupants, either directly by burning them up, or indirectly by forcing them to flee and die of exposure in the blizzard. On the other hand, if the fire goes out, they will freeze even though they are in the cabin. The key, then, is adequate respect for and control of the fire.

Anger can be very destructive or extremely useful. So often anger is misused and that's why it's gotten a bad rap; however, it does have its appropriate place—it can help mobilize us toward healthy action. Remember, anger is a communicable attribute of God; He has given it to us for a purpose.

Handling Your Anger
Part 1

What should you do when you become angry? How should you respond when someone snaps at you and suddenly you feel hurt, your jaw tenses, and angry retorts flash through your mind?

I have outlined a step-by-step procedure that is helpful for the times when you become angry, hostile, or upset:

1. Recognize Your Feelings

The first step is to get in touch with your feelings of hurt, displeasure, or anger. For many people this is not a problem because they are acutely aware of their feelings. However, for others this step is the most important one. They may be like Jan, the woman described in chapter 1, who contemplated jumping off an 18-story bridge. She had repressed her feelings of anger for so long that the only manifestation was that she felt funny and confused. Only after we had spent almost 30 minutes reconstructing the events that led to this sense of confusion did she remember the original incident and some minuscule feelings.

I have worked with several individuals like Jan who needed months of therapy for them to get in touch with their feelings. In a therapy session, typically we would examine the manifestations of what I thought might be anger, and then we would work back to the initial incident. Sometimes even after all that, they still wouldn't feel anything. We would then see how they handled the situation to discover what kinds of feelings might have produced their behavior. At other times we would figure out what other people might feel in a similar situation.

I usually have to search for and use exactly the right word to describe their feelings. For example, if I use a word like *mad*, *angry*, or *furious*, they often reject it. However, if I use the word *annoyed*, they might accept it. Jan always rejected the word *anger*, but some of the time she could identify "slight feelings of irritation." We would then work with "feelings of irritation" in applying the principles of this book. By these means, then, we were able to fan the embers of her feelings until they became stronger.

At this point in the proceedings, *do not judge* the cause of the feeling, or whether the feeling is reasonable, or is right or wrong. For now you are only identifying the *presence* of any hurt or angry feelings. This step can be compared to looking at the temperature gauge on the dashboard of your car; you aren't determining the cause of the overheated engine, but are only becoming aware of the fact that it is overheated.

While you are getting in touch with your feelings, evaluate whether you are a little upset, moderately upset, or very upset. This will help serve as an important clue later on as to the action you may need to take. If you aren't aware of the degree of your anger, you may find yourself overreacting to minor issues or even under-reacting to major ones.

2. Delay Taking Any Action

Nehemiah said, "I was very angry when I heard their cry and these words. *I thought it over* and then rebuked the nobles and officials" (Nehemiah 5:6,7 AMP, emphasis added). Here Nehemiah was able to get in touch with his feelings and then to think through the situation. Then he delayed taking any action until he had *thought through* the situation and had *control over what he would say and do.* This step is akin to the proverbial "counting to ten," or, as Thomas Jefferson said, "When angry, count ten before you speak; if very angry, an hundred."[61] This step should only take a brief period of time. Sometimes it may take only seconds or minutes, but in some cases it may take hours or possibly days. However, it is critical to do this as soon as possible so you do not lose touch with the problem.

One might rightfully ask, "What is the difference between someone who 'delays taking any action' and 'the suppressor'?" It is a matter of time, of how much is suppressed, and of how the situation is ultimately handled. In this step I am advocating restraining your feelings and actions for a brief period of time before taking definitive action. On the other hand, "the suppressor" chronically buries his feelings, never constructively dealing with them, so that they pile up. In contrast to both of these, "the aggressor" responds to his feelings impulsively and destructively, producing carnage.

The Bible encourages us not to be hasty in dealing with our anger. Proverbs 29:11 says, "A fool gives full vent to his anger, but a wise man quietly holds it back" (RSV). In the Amplified Bible this verse says, "A [self-confident] fool utters all his anger, but a wise man holds it back and stills it."

I have already stated that I would not take any action at this stage in the proceedings. However, there are two exceptions: the first is where you need to *tag the situation,* and the second is when you need to *notify innocent bystanders.*

a. Tag the Situation

If you find yourself in a situation in which you suddenly have some angry feelings that aren't altogether clear to you yet and *someone asks you* if you're upset, you might be tempted to say, "No, it didn't bother me." If in reality you were bothered, making such a statement would be dishonest, making it more difficult to deal with the incident with that person later on, should the need arise.

It would be better to say something like, "Yes, I am upset, but I'll have to think it through before I say anything more about it." Or you might "tag" the situation by saying, "Something about that bothers me, but it's not clear to me yet. Maybe when I've had a chance to think it over we can talk about it." Tagging the situation marks it as a problem to you and the other person, but clarifies that you are consciously deferring any definitive action. It also alerts the other person to think about what had just happened, thus decreasing the chance that he will forget about it, which might further anger you, making the matter more difficult to deal with later on.

If you don't tag the situation verbally, it is crucial that you at least tag it in your mind. That way, if there are some urgent tasks at hand when you become aware that something is bothering you, you will have pinned the problem down in your mind and committed yourself to coming back to deal with it later. If you don't tag the situation, it is possible that you will forget what it was that caused you to feel upset. Then if you feel vaguely upset later, you won't know why, and you may not be able to resolve the problem. Forgetting to tag situations, over time, can cause all kinds of havoc and can add to your unresolved anger fund.

Several months ago my wife suggested that I take over a certain responsibility around the house that she had been handling up to that time. Immediately I became aware of the fact that I was irritated and a score of considerations rapidly passed through my mind: *Does she have a legitimate basis for asking me to do this? I do so many other things; I'm so busy right now with my schedule, and so on and so forth.* Because my wife can read my facial expressions, she asked, "Did that bother you?" I responded, "Yes, it upset me."

Thus I tagged the situation, and while I honestly thought I would be able to sort out my feelings fairly quickly, it took at least another ten minutes for my thoughts to clarify. When they were clarified, I could express my feelings, and we were able to work through the problem. In this situation I followed the first two steps in dealing with anger: I recognized my feelings of displeasure, and though I suppressed taking any action, I did tag the situation.

b. Notify Innocent Bystanders

One additional step you may want to take while delaying taking action is to notify innocent bystanders when something is bothering you. For example, if you have had a very traumatic day at work and you come home with a lot of things on your mind, it is wise to inform your family of that fact and to ask them to "give you some room." When you let them know that they are not the ones who are troubling you, they are less likely to conjure up a lot of incorrect assumptions about your behavior. By notifying others they will realize they are not responsible for your bad mood, and thus they are more likely to be helpful, even if it means doing nothing more than staying out of your way.

However, informing innocent bystanders of your dilemma never gives you license to take out your frustrations on them. Also, if asking your family for "room" occurs very frequently, you may need to take a careful look as to why this is occurring so often and the effects this pattern is having on your family.

It also pays to remember that timing is very important in dealing with emotional issues. I've already mentioned that it is essential to wait before taking action until you have thought through the situation and have adequate control of both your words and actions. I want to emphasize that I am not saying you must have control of *all* of your feelings. In fact, at times it is useful to take action when there are still some feelings present, because they can motivate you to take necessary action.

3. Pray for Guidance

"Then Hezekiah took the letter [telling of threats by an ungodly enemy] from the hand of the messengers and read it, and he went up to the house of the LORD and *spread it out before the LORD. And...prayed*" (2 Kings 19:14, emphasis added). When Hezekiah was threatened, he took the matter to God in prayer and asked for help.

At any point in the sequence of dealing with anger it is appropriate to ask the Lord for understanding, guidance, and wisdom so that you will handle the conflict in a manner most pleasing to Him. I don't believe that a person necessarily has to pray specifically in each and every quandary that arises, but I do believe this should be the general desire of the heart. On the other hand, there may be occasions when a person will need to draw away, like Hezekiah did, to pray specifically about a situation.

4. Identify the True Cause of Your Anger

What is it that is making you feel so upset? What is causing your anger? What is being threatened? Answering these questions is the next step.

Many times the cause of the anger is obvious, so this step is no problem at all. However, people who have difficulty understanding and dealing with their feelings may have considerable difficulty with this step. If you get angry at your 10-year-old son for leaving his bike in the driveway, you need to consider whether the true cause of your anger is the boss who chewed you out at work, or the man who cut you off on the freeway. It is so easy for anger to be displaced upon someone or something with whom it is safer to take out that bottled-up feeling. I'm sure you are familiar with the following chain reaction: The boss yelled at his employee, who then got angry at his wife, who then took it out on her son, who then kicked the dog.

This pattern of taking out one's anger on a weaker creature is not unique to human beings; it has even been documented in laboratory animals. Probably the first recorded incident of the displacement of anger onto a defenseless animal is found in Numbers 22, when Balaam became angry at his donkey instead of realizing that he was upset at God.

I know of people who are stymied at this step because they have great difficulty in figuring out what made them so angry. Each of them, in his or her own way, has to pause to determine the sequence of events leading up to the incident that caused the anger. One person may need to write notes on a piece of paper until the issues are clarified. Another may need to talk over the problem with a close friend. Still another may need professional help to identify the source of his angry feelings. But whatever it takes to do the job, you cannot proceed any further until the cause of the displeasure, hurt, or anger is identified.

In real-life situations there is often more than one issue to which we must respond. One of my patients was told, by her mother, "That certainly is a beautiful dress, even if you are overweight." Here the mother was sending out two distinctly different messages in one sentence. Dealing with only one message is quite inadequate and causes all sorts of havoc. The daughter has to separate the contradictory messages, both the compliment and the insult. She must then decide if and how she wants to respond to both parts of this message. She might say, "Thanks for the compliment about the dress, but your comment about my weight really irritated me." From that point on they can deal with either or both of the issues.

In this illustration, the fact that there are two different issues is obvious. Unfortunately, most situations are not quite as obvious. When several messages are being sent and when they are more subtle than the ones I just gave in the above illustration, sorting them out and dealing with each one can become a difficult process.

5. Evaluate Whether Your Anger Is Legitimate

In Jonah 4:9, God said to Jonah, "Do you have good reason to be angry...?" God was questioning Jonah as to whether he had an adequate basis for his angry feelings. It turned out that Jonah didn't have a just cause for his anger.

This reminds me of the day my 13-year-old son came whizzing past me in the breakfast room and greeted me with the words, "Hi, Chubby." He wasn't even out of the room before I could sense that I was starting to feel very angry. I was just about ready to say something when I realized that there was some truth in what he had just said, so I delayed taking any action.

As I thought about it, I became aware that it was the legitimacy of the statement that made it hurt. What made me so mad was the fact that he was right! I had been telling myself for six months that I needed to reduce my weight. Thus I concluded that my son was right and that I had no legitimate basis for getting upset with him, and soon my feelings of anger quickly subsided. If my son had had a habit of saying things like that it would have been a different matter, but this had been the only time he had ever made such a comment, so I could let it pass.

It is interesting to note that within a week a colleague of mine at work said to me, "You ought to lose some weight, Dwight." I agreed with him, saying, "You know, you're right." And this feeling of displeasure with my weight spurred me on to losing 20 pounds.

6. Determine a Course of Action

Let's look at Nehemiah 5:6,7 again: "I [Nehemiah] was very angry when I heard their cry and these words. I thought it over and then rebuked the nobles and officials" (AMP). Here we see Nehemiah get in touch with his feelings, think through the situation, and then take the appropriate action—in this case he rebuked the rich leaders who were charging such exorbitant interest that they were forcing the people of Israel into slavery.

It is possible that at any of the steps we have discussed thus far, you may have been able to resolve your feelings of anger. For instance, if you did not have a legitimate issue, you could resolve the problem at that step. However, if the problem has not been resolved, then the time has come for you to determine a course of action that you will need to take to handle your feelings constructively. Below I list eight different possible courses of action. If you want to be able to handle anger maturely, you will need to become proficient with *each* one of these approaches.

a. Confront When Necessary

Anyone who really cares about people's feelings finds confrontation difficult, but a mature person will confront when it is necessary. In 2 Corinthians 2:4, Paul shares with his readers how he felt about having to confront them: "Oh, how I hated to write that letter! It almost broke my heart and I tell you honestly that I cried over it. I didn't want to hurt you, but I had to show you how very much I loved you and cared about what was happening to you" (TLB).

It is worthwhile here to take a brief look at the context of the previously quoted verse about anger, Ephesians 4:26, noting particularly verses 25-27,32: "Therefore, laying aside falsehood, speak truth, each one of you, with his neighbor, for we are members of one another. Be angry, and yet do not sin; do not let the sun go down on your anger, and do not give the devil an opportunity....be kind to one another, tender-hearted, forgiving each other." First there is the call to drop the mask of falsehood and to speak the truth, being honest with each other. Then the writer states that though anger is called for in some situations, we must not let it lead to sin. He then goes on to tell us to be kind and tenderhearted, and to forgive each other.

At first glance these instructions may appear to contradict each other, but when seen in the light of dealing honestly with anger, the entire perspective changes. Speaking the truth in love often necessitates confrontation, and sometimes this confrontation must take place before one can be forgiving. David Augsburger has referred to such confronting as "truthing it in love."[62]

There are many examples of confrontation in the Scriptures. Probably the first example that comes to mind is when Jesus spoke sharply to the Pharisees in Mark 7. It is interesting to note that even Jesus' disciples couldn't understand His remarks to the religious leaders, and on one occasion they even rebuked Him, saying, "You offended the Pharisees by that remark" (Matthew 15:12 TLB). But Jesus did not retract His statement because He had fully intended to confront the Pharisees.

Jesus also rebuked Peter sharply in Matthew 16:23, saying, "Get behind Me, Satan!" We find that Paul "had great dissension and debate" with some men from Judea regarding religious customs (Acts 15:2). Paul also opposed Peter "to his face" because Peter was wrong on a certain issue (Galatians 2:11).

Confrontation isn't necessarily a hostile, painful experience; it can be done in a tender and forgiving manner. One example of this kind of confrontation is the way Jesus treated the adulterous woman whom the Pharisees wanted to stone to death. Jesus said to the woman, "Go and sin no more" (John 8:11 TLB). He acknowledged the fact that she had been sinning, then simply and kindly told her to leave her sinful ways.

Jesus had a similarly gentle confrontation with the woman He met at the well in John chapter 4. She was living with a man to whom she wasn't married. He didn't just say that what she was doing was wrong, but He also introduced her to a new way of life. Genuine confrontation, "truthing it in love," is not attacking another person, but caring enough about the person and the relationship to talk directly to him. Whenever possible, it is best that confrontation be done in private. If a problem has developed between you and another person, endeavor to resolve it between the two of you alone, without involving others. Proverbs 25:8,9 speaks tellingly to our lawsuit-prone society: "Do not go out hastily to argue your case; otherwise, what will you do in the end, when your neighbor puts you to shame? Argue your case with your neighbor, and do not reveal the secret of another." Matthew 18:15 says, "If a brother sins against you, go to him privately and confront him with his fault" (TLB).

There are several exceptions to this. First, if others have observed the conflict or were in some way involved, the problem may need to be resolved with these individuals present. Another time that you may want to involve others is if a person refuses to deal with you, yet you feel that an important issue is at stake that requires resolution. The presence of another is valuable if you are fearful of being misquoted, or you are concerned about your own safety, or you just need moral support. Immediately after Matthew 18:15, which we just quoted, we read: "If he [the brother who sins against you] listens and confesses it, you have won back a brother. But if not, then take one or two others with you and go back to him again, proving everything you say by these witnesses. If he still refuses to listen, then take your case to the church" (verses 16,17 TLB). Though it is preferable not to involve others, there are some occasions when it is necessary.

There are three general ways to confront people: 1) to inform; 2) to share your primary feelings; and 3) to rebuke in love.

1) To Inform: On January 29, 1979, an Air Force sergeant traveling from California to Colorado spent more money than anticipated on car repairs. Consequently, he ran out of gas and money in Raton, New Mexico. Although he had money in his checking account, the banks, gas stations, and motels refused his personal checks. So the sergeant obediently went back to his disabled car, where he spent the night in subfreezing weather. Had the police department or others in the town been informed of his plight, they would have made provisions for him, as they had for others in the past. But the sergeant's failure to inform the townspeople of his situation cost him his feet, which had to be amputated because they were so badly frostbitten. The residents of the town were deeply grieved when they heard the news. This incident graphically illustrates the extent to which people can be hurt simply because they fail to adequately inform others of their situation.

We often fail to simply inform another person clearly and honestly about our feelings on an issue. For example, the simple statement, "You're stepping on my foot" is usually the best way to inform a person in a crowded elevator that he is hurting you and that you would like him to move. The person may not even be aware that he is stepping on your foot unless you quietly inform him of the fact. To angrily snap, "You're stepping on my foot, you clod!" would most likely provoke an angry response and lead to a negative situation. Another example of informing someone about your feelings is saying to the person who cuts in front of you, "Excuse me, the line forms over there." Even if the person has deliberately taken advantage of you, usually a simple statement like this resolves the situation without worsening it.

When we feel something strongly, it is up to us to express it. *We are asking for all kinds of trouble if we assume that the other person knows how strongly we feel, unless we actually put it into words and express our feelings directly to the person involved.*

In the past, my wife, Betty, and I have been guilty of inadequately informing each other of our feelings, and we continue to find it necessary to work on this area of our marriage. I recall an incident that made us acutely aware of the need to share our feelings. I was extremely busy with a full practice and was on many hospital-related and church-related committees. Often I would leave home early in the morning before the family had breakfast and would arrive home late at night after everyone was in bed. No doubt I was in error for being so busy, and for that reason I was not tuned in to Betty's needs. Betty, on the other hand, not wanting to bother me with her needs because I was so busy, only hinted quietly of her need to talk with me—hints that I honestly didn't hear. If I had received her messages more clearly, I would have dropped anything to be of help to her, but I had no idea how much she was hurting, and she didn't know how to inform me.

One day a friend confronted Betty with her responsibility to inform me of her turmoil, even if it meant making an appointment with me in my office. Finally she wrote me a note and left it on my desk to open the channels of communication. Unfortunately she went through some very painful weeks before she informed me, and by that time the situation had created some deep hurts for both of us. Had I sensed my wife's feelings or had she informed me earlier, it would have saved both of us a lot of grief.

2) To Share Your Primary Feelings: The second way to confront is to *share your primary feelings.* Anger itself is actually a *secondary* feeling—a reaction to some insult, threat, or put-down, or a response of frustration when our wishes or needs aren't met. The *primary* feeling is usually hurt, intimidation, belittlement, fear, or frustration, to name a few typical ones. For example, if someone stomps on your foot, you first feel pain, which is followed by anger. Pain is the primary feeling, and anger the secondary feeling. Each step in this God-given process is vital. The primary feeling of pain is the protective warning signal. The secondary feeling, anger, enables you to take protective actions against the offender. One of the most constructive ways of dealing with anger is to get in touch with the primary feeling and then to share this feeling with the person you need to confront.

This is best exemplified by sending an "I feel" message. "I feel" messages are a beautiful way of sharing how you feel, and they often help everyone involved to get in touch with their primary feelings. Below are some examples of "blaming you" messages, as contrasted to "I feel" messages.

"Blaming You" Message	**"I Feel" Message**
1. You're making me mad because you're paying so much attention to Mary.	1. I'm feeling ignored.

"Blaming You" Message	**"I Feel" Message**
2. You're deliberately leaving me behind.	2. I feel disappointed that I can't go too.
3. You always blame me for everything that goes wrong.	3. I get the feeling that I'm being blamed for that.
4. You're always putting me down.	4. I feel put down.
5. Why are you interrogating me again?	5. I feel like I'm being interrogated.

"Blaming you" messages usually begin with the word "you" and include an accusation. They frequently assume to know the intent, motivation, or feelings of the other person. For example, "You're deliberately leaving me behind" assumes to know the motive of the other person's actions. Even if the "blaming you" message is correct, it is usually difficult to defend. Such messages come off as being judgmental, critical, attacking, and final, giving no room for the other person to respond or provide clarification. They tend to raise the hostilities and defenses of the other person. Only the extremely mature person can receive a "blaming you" message and turn it into a constructive interaction.

During my psychiatric residency, I was eating lunch once with several colleagues when my boss sat down and joined us. During the course of the conversation he said something that really hurt. In my mind I quickly went through the steps mentioned earlier, and within about two seconds I was aware of intense hurt and angry feelings, and

I knew I needed to confront him. I decided to send off the briefest of "I feel" messages, and said just two words—"That hurts." For about a minute, you could have heard a pin drop at that table. The topic of conversation changed, but later I sought him out to share in greater depth my honest feelings with him and to ask him some specific questions regarding his. The problem was resolved between us.

Another incident that I resolved by sending an "I feel" message occurred at about the same period of time. This situation involved a colleague of mine and a supervising psychiatrist. On past occasions it had appeared to me that this supervisor had torn into other residents unmercifully. Then came a conversation in which he seemed to be throwing out disguised criticisms at my colleague and me because we hadn't found more problem cases to discuss with him. I certainly didn't want him to tear into me, but neither did I like the anger I was beginning to feel toward him. So I said, "I'm beginning to feel uncomfortable," and then said nothing for awhile. There was dead silence for probably 30 or 40 seconds, after which he said, "Now I'm beginning to feel uncomfortable." I still said nothing further, and then he quickly interjected, "I didn't mean any criticism by what I said." Thus the problem was resolved by sending an "I feel" message. I might add that from that point onward everything went well, without any subtly critical comments from the supervisor.

David Augsburger says in his book, *Caring Enough to Confront*, "Avoiding honest statements of real feelings and viewpoints is often considered kindness, thoughtfulness, or generosity. More often it is the most cruel thing I can do to others. It is a kind of benevolent lying."[63]

3) To Rebuke in Love: The third and strongest way to confront is to *rebuke in love.* Here you are telling the person directly that what he is saying or doing is inappropriate, but note that the rebuke is done with love, as opposed to being aggressive. Because you care about the person you are rebuking, the aim of rebuking in love is reconciliation. You may dislike or even hate what the person is doing, but you make it clear to the person that you care about him. Proverbs 27:5,6 says, "Open rebuke is better than hidden love! Wounds from a friend are better than kisses from an enemy!" (TLB). As I mentioned earlier, the priest Eli probably sinned because "he did not rebuke" his sons (1 Samuel 3:13). All he did was meekly question them when they disregarded God's laws of worship.

One word of warning: Some people are afraid of confrontations because they don't know if they will be able to control their anger. For most people, learning to confront others is very uncomfortable at first. Despite the disconcerting feelings we might have when we approach a confrontation, we need to keep in mind that if we have gone through the steps for handling our anger properly, we most likely won't say or do anything we will regret later. However, if you feel violently angry, you may have to put off confrontation and get some help, perhaps even professional help, so that you will be able to confront the other person without verbally or physically attacking him.

Don't use your uncomfortable feelings as an excuse for avoiding confrontation. As we learned earlier, the cost of failing to confront someone can be very great. It is far better to try to resolve the situation (using the steps I've outlined) than to let it get worse with the passage of time. When you work to resolve the problem, usually you will find yourself rewarded with a restored friendship and peace of mind.

Handling Your Anger
Part 2

In the previous chapter I began giving a set of practical steps for handling specific situations that cause you to feel hurt or angry. (This entire sequence is shown on Illustration 7, which is on pages 94–95.) First you need to recognize your feelings, and then you should delay taking any action until you have thought through the problem and have full control of your words and actions. Prayer for guidance is always appropriate. From there you need to identify the true cause of your anger and see if it has a legitimate basis. Only then do you decide on a course of action. We just finished discussing confrontation, the first of 8 specific actions that one might take.

We will now continue looking at specific actions that you may need to take in any anger producing situation.

b. Set Limits on Behavior (Boundaries)

Kristine, a 31-year-old, sought my help because of depression. She has two boys, ages eight and ten, with

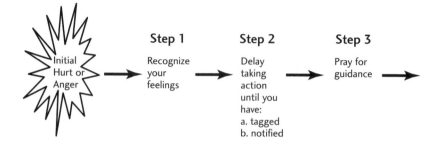

Steps in Dealing with Anger
Illustration 7

whom she is frequently angry. For example, John, the 10-year-old, often leaves his bicycle parked just outside the back door so that others have to walk around it. Several times, Kristine has stumbled over it. Kristine is aware of her anger over this and she has confronted John, but only by yelling and screaming, which doesn't seem to accomplish very much.

One week we talked about the terms "setting limits" and "establishing consequences." By the term "setting limits" I mean determining the difference between what behavior is acceptable and what is not acceptable. By the term "establishing consequences" I mean making a clear

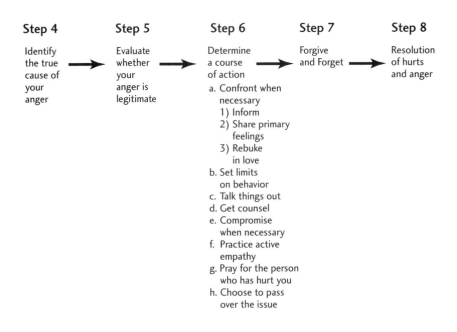

Step 4	Step 5	Step 6	Step 7	Step 8
Identify the true cause of your anger	Evaluate whether your anger is legitimate	Determine a course of action	Forgive and Forget	Resolution of hurts and anger

		a. Confront when necessary
		  1) Inform
		  2) Share primary feelings
		  3) Rebuke in love
		b. Set limits on behavior
		c. Talk things out
		d. Get counsel
		e. Compromise when necessary
		f. Practice active empathy
		g. Pray for the person who has hurt you
		h. Choose to pass over the issue		

statement of what would happen if an unacceptable behavior occurred. Guess what happened? The very next day Kristine was carrying a large box from the house to the garage, and she didn't see John's bike blocking the back door. She stumbled and dropped the box. Her adrenaline surged, and she yelled at John.

Then Kristine remembered our session the day before. She cooled down and firmly called John. She explained what had just happened and how she might have injured herself or damaged the items in the box. Then she clearly and firmly told John that she would take the box to the garage and that she expected the bike to be removed by the time she returned. If it wasn't removed, she would remove it; and if she ever found his bike lying outside the door, it would be locked up for a week. This would mean he would have to walk a mile to and from school and wouldn't be able to ride his bike after school—an activity that was very important to him.

As Kristine walked to the garage, she was amazed at how quickly her angry feelings had subsided. Normally such an episode would have ruined the rest of her day, and possibly also the rest of her family's day. When she returned to the house the bike was gone, and it never blocked the back door again. Kristine was astonished at how well this approach had resolved the problem, as compared to her previous habit of yelling. She had established a limit on John's behavior with predetermined consequences, and it had worked.

Limit-setting can be used in any situation in which a person has the right and/or responsibility to establish limits, rules, or criteria. It can also be used when another person's behavior encroaches on your rightful area of control. This is especially applicable to parents, teachers, and employers, but limit-setting can be used in all kinds of relationships. Keep in mind, however, that when you set limits, the rules must be fair and consistently applied, all parties should know the consequences before the infraction is done, and you must follow through on the consequences even when you are tempted to overlook the infraction "just this one time."

In most instances it isn't wise to establish the consequences after the offense. For example, if Kristine had stumbled on John's bike and had locked it up without warning him, he might have had legitimate reason to feel that his mother was being unfair. Instead, she gave him enough time to remove his bike and avoid the consequences. Furthermore, she let him know that the consequences would be applied immediately if he ever broke the rule again.

For further help in setting limits I would suggest the following books: *Boundaries: When to Say Yes, When to Say No, To Take Control of Your Life,* and *Boundaries with Kids.*[64]

c. Talk Things Out

Talking things out can also serve as a type of catharsis. It includes the idea of cleansing or purging. Since talk can allow for a healthy release of ideas and feelings, especially the painful ones, this step is appropriate anywhere in the sequence because some people may need to get the issues and their feelings exposed before they can take any other action.

Usually catharsis is thought of as talking things out in the presence of someone who knows how to listen empathically. In fact, it has been found that the deeper the level of disclosure to another, the more one's own well-being is improved.[65]

The Scriptures are full of examples of catharsis. Job, the Psalms, and Lamentations all illustrate a godly person pouring out his feelings to God. Sharing your deepest feelings to God in prayer is an excellent means of catharsis. However, I have seen people get things out of their system by writing a letter, even if they never mail it. Others may put their thoughts on paper, talk to themselves in private, or even tape-record their feelings. A trusted friend may be invaluable at this time. I have seen many individuals, especially those who have little awareness of their feelings, greatly benefit from just being able to express them—often for the first time. In some instances catharsis is all that is needed to dissipate hurt and angry feelings. In other situations, however, it is only one of several steps that need to be taken.

Carefully performed studies now validate the beneficial effects of being able to express your negative feelings: improved immune system function, reduction in blood pressure, fewer visits to health providers, lower medical expenses, and shorter hospital stays.[66] This includes sharing one's feelings—whether it is to an individual, in a diary, or as part of a religious confession.[67]

However, there is a limit to catharsis. It can be valuable up to a certain point, but if you get stuck there it can become destructive. Job ventilated his anguish to his friends and God from chapter 3 through 37 of the book of Job. Then in chapter 38 God said, in essence, "Job, that's enough." Continued catharsis can, at some point, actually increase the individual's pent-up anger and lead to inappropriate aggressive behaviors.[68]

d. Get Counsel

Another way to handle negative feelings is to seek counsel. At times all of us find ourselves in need of someone with whom we can talk over a problem. This person need not be a professional; sometimes a friend, spouse, or peer who can help clarify issues and give objectivity to a problem is all that we need. In any case, this person should be emotionally mature, a good listener, and not be prone to give quick answers. He should be someone who won't gossip about your problem or use it against you. However, some people may need to get counsel from a professional. This is especially true of a person who might lose control of himself if he started getting in touch with his anger or other deep feelings. As mentioned previously, praying is certainly advisable at any time and can be an invaluable means of getting counsel from God, the Great Counselor (see James 1:5).

e. Compromise When Necessary

When we get angry, seldom are we 100 percent right and the other person 100 percent wrong. Typically there are multiple factors causing the problem and several different ways to view the situation. After we have gone through some of the steps for handling anger, particularly the step of confrontation, we often become aware of the other person's feelings, and suddenly we can see the situation from a different perspective. We may then be faced with the need to compromise. The ability to compromise is an integral characteristic of the emotionally and spiritually mature person (see Acts 15:1-29). While we don't want our feelings to be ignored and trampled underfoot, neither do we want to do the same to the other person. It is characteristic of the immature person to either demand his own way or to perpetually give in. David Augsburger writes:

> Compromise is a gift to human relationships. We move forward on the basis of thoughtful, careful consensus and compromise in most decisions in conflict. But it calls for at least a partial sacrifice of

deeply held views and goals...to reach...agreement. Working through differences by giving clear messages of "I care" and "I want," which both care and confront, is most helpful.

This is interpersonal communication at its best. Caring—I want to stay in respectful relationships with you, and I want you to know where I stand and what I am feeling, needing, valuing and wanting. ...These are the two arms of genuine relationship: confrontation with truth; affirmation with love.[69]

f. Practice Active Empathy

Empathy is insightful awareness into the emotions and behavior of another person. It means we "walk in their moccasins"; we try to see and feel the world through their eyes. I use the term "active empathy," which emphasizes the need for effort. We all tend to have myopia; that is, we are focused on our own little world—our needs, feelings, and wishes. We seldom give even equal attention to another person's perspective, trying to see the world through their eyes.

When conflict occurs, I believe it can be exceedingly useful to actively endeavor to see the situation through the other person's eyes and to try to sense their feelings. We might evaluate how we would respond if we came from the other person's background and had their hurts. Sometimes looking for the reasons behind the other person's behavior can be helpful.[70] It can be an eye-opener that can help us relate to the person with more compassion. In fact, the more empathic we are, the less likely it is that we will get angry in the first place.[71]

Christ showed inexplicable empathy when He was on the cross, praying, "Forgive them; for they do not know what they are doing" (Luke 23:34).

g. Pray for the Person Who Has Hurt You

When Stephen was being stoned for his faith he prayed, "Lord, do not hold this sin against them!" (Acts 7:60). Christ tells us to "bless them that curse you, and pray for them which despitefully use you" (Luke 6:28 KJV).

I don't know about you, but I find it hard to hold a grudge against someone I am actively praying for. Admittedly, this takes a lot of maturity. It does not negate all that I have said previously about the need to confront or set limits, however. More will be said about this in chapter 12.

h. Choose to Pass Over the Issue

At times we must learn to pass over the issue. This is not suppression or repression, which is denying the existence of a significant problem and burying any accompanying feelings. Passing over an issue involves a *full awareness* of the injury done to us and a deliberate willingness to *completely* drop the charges against the person who has hurt us. We choose to relinquish the charges. It means that we *hold no grudges*—that we are willing to forgive so that we can move toward forgetting.

Two good reasons for passing over the issue are: 1) realizing we don't have a good enough case against the other person; and 2) recognizing that it's not worth the emotional expense to us and the other person to press charges. In such cases, passing over the issue may be the best possible solution to the problem, both for ourselves and for the other person.

Something Os Guinness says can help us pass over issues: "The key is to realize that no one is primarily responsible to God for what other people *have done* to him, whether through actions or teaching; the other people are responsible to God for this. But each person is responsible to God for what he has *done with* what others have done to him."[72]

For example, I have found that I can choose whether to react with or without anger to a scratch or dent somebody left on my car. Sure, I don't like scratches on my car, but I also realize that a car is only a material possession and is not worth the emotional expense. That doesn't mean that I would never try to get the party at fault to pay for the damages. It merely means that there are times when I may choose to pass over the anger-producing problem. I am also finding that as I become more mature I am able to pass over more conflicts.

One night as I started to back out of the parking lot at work, I noticed that one headlight wasn't working. I got out of the car to see why, and discovered that it was smashed. The car parked in front of me had a high bumper that could easily have smashed the headlight. But when I thought about what a hassle it would be to try to find the owner and to confront him, I chose to drop the issue. I drove home, and, the next day, went to a store and paid a few dollars for another light to replace the damaged one. That was a bargain in comparison to the time and emotional energy the problem might otherwise have cost.

Several years ago we bought a toilet seat from a large department store. It was guaranteed, in writing, never to break. There was just one problem: it kept breaking. Several times we went back to have it replaced, but it was always a struggle to get the store to honor its guarantee. Eventually we got to the point where we decided it just wasn't worth the emotional price tag to fight the store, so we passed over the issue and let the matter drop.

I've worked in county hospitals and have seen many things I don't like. On some matters I took a stand, but on others I decided that, for me, it wasn't worth the price involved to take a stand even though injustices were being committed. When it comes to anger-producing situations, we must decide which issues we will take a stand on. We don't want to take a stand on every single one, or we will become cynical and hostile after awhile. We will talk more about this in chapter 12.

Carol Tavris writes in *Anger: The Misunderstood Emotion,* "There are other battles to fight....This one wasn't worth it to me. For some of the large indignities of life, the best remedy is direct action. For the small indignities, the best remedy is a Charlie Chaplin movie. The hard part is knowing the difference."[73]

We must choose our battles. The world is filled with injustices and irritants. Jesus chose to deal with the Pharisees at certain times, but there were other times that He didn't. There were some issues Jesus legitimately could have fought, such as slavery. But He chose not to confront this issue. During His time on earth, Israel was occupied by Roman soldiers, but He chose not to take a stand against that.

Proverbs 19:11 says, "The discretion of a man deferreth his anger; and *it is his glory to pass over a transgression*" (KJV, emphasis added). First Peter 2:23 says Christ "never answered back when insulted; when he suffered he did not threaten to get even; he left his case in the hands of God who always judges fairly" (TLB). Jesus could accept unjust treatment because He knew that God would someday judge the entire situation righteously. He could leave problems in God's hands.

7. Forgive and Forget

The final step in dealing with anger—and perhaps the most crucial one—is to forgive and forget. Matthew 6:15 warns, " If you do not forgive others their trespasses [their reckless and willful sins, leaving them, letting them go and giving up resentment] neither will your Father forgive you your trespasses" (AMP).

Many of us have misconceptions about what forgiveness really is. When trying to forgive someone, we try to talk ourselves into thinking that what the other person did wasn't really wrong, or that he didn't really mean to do it, or that we overreacted. There are times when we need to fully recognize that what the other person did was definitely wrong, but that we will still forgive him, so that we can move toward forgetting—no matter how much he has hurt us.

Forgiving means that we actively choose to give up our grudge despite the severity of the injustice done to us. It doesn't mean that we say, "That didn't hurt me" or, "It didn't really matter." Some things may hurt very much and we must not deny that fact, but after fully recognizing the hurt, we should choose to forgive. Forgiving doesn't mean that the party at fault doesn't need to suffer the consequences of his actions. You can forgive someone and still allow justice to be administered. For example, if a drunken driver kills your child, it is appropriate that legal action be taken against him. This is necessary not only for your family's sake, but also for the driver's and society's sake.

To bring this a little closer to home, let's say that your child is aware that you are angry at him for something he has done. He admits he was wrong and asks your forgiveness. If he is sincere, I believe it is your responsibility to forgive him. This doesn't mean that you don't have to discipline him, but it does mean that after you have discussed the problem with him and both of you have had the opportunity to share your feelings, you should give up your feelings of anger.

Usually we come to this step of forgiving and forgetting after we have taken some or many of the previous steps we've discussed for dealing with anger. If we don't ultimately forgive the person and try to forget the situation, there are going to be repercussions in our own lives. For example, we often have the distorted notion that the other person suffers when we hold a grudge against him. Usually just the opposite is true: When you hold a grudge, often the other person doesn't even know about it, and even if he does, he probably doesn't care! The only person who is being hurt is you. Holding a grudge and refusing to forgive is like licking your emotional wounds, which you may instinctively enjoy, but what you must realize is that you will suffer greatly because of the weight of the grudge you are holding.

It's been said that holding a grudge or being filled with resentment is like drinking poison and wishing the other person would die. I am told that when you catch a shark, as you try to bring it into the boat it will become so enraged that it will bite anything. In fact, it may flap around and take a big bite out of its own tail. This, in a sense, is what happens to us when we hold on to our anger and resentment.

Even if the problem becomes buried in our subconscious or unconscious mind so that we aren't even aware of it, it will continue to extract an emotional toll. And no one else can be blamed for that part of the emotional weight; we have put it upon ourselves. More will be said about this in chapter 12.

A Final Word

It is quickly apparent that handling anger constructively is a more complicated and drawn-out procedure then handling anger destructively. It takes more time, effort, and skill. However, once you have learned the skills, it will take less and less energy to implement them.

Dealing with anger is a lot like learning to drive a car or master a foreign language. It's always hard work at first and you make a lot of mistakes, but eventually it becomes second nature—you hardly need to think about it.

It is important to point out that *each* of the skills discussed will be necessary for you to use at one time or another. The particular means you choose will depend on the situation and your ability to think it through and select the *best* course of action. You must be familiar with and able to use each of these skills or you will run into difficulty. Not being able to draw on a particular skill when it is needed is a gigantic handicap.

This entire process of handling anger constructively in those tense moments when you are emotionally upset can be summed up with the following two scripture passages—one from the Old Testament, and one from the New.

Leviticus 19:17,18 says, "Don't hate your brother. Rebuke anyone who sins; don't let him get away with it, or you will be equally guilty. Don't seek vengeance. Don't bear a grudge; but love your neighbor as yourself, for I am Jehovah" (TLB).

I've already quoted Ephesians 4:25-27,32; nevertheless, I feel that its message bears repeating. "Therefore, laying aside falsehood, speak truth, each one of you, with his neighbor, for we are members of one another. Be angry, and yet do not sin; do not let the sun go down on your anger, and do not give the devil an opportunity....be kind to one another, tender-hearted, forgiving each other, just as God in Christ also has forgiven you."

Practice What You Know

Remember Jan, the college student described in chapter 1 who contemplated jumping off the 18-story bridge? How can we help someone as numb as Jan apply the principles we have been describing? This task could be compared to trying to fan into flame the embers of a fire—you have to gently blow on them to get them to glow a little brighter, hoping that eventually the fire will catch.

The Numb Person

People like Jan need help getting in touch with those faint feelings that are barely perceptible. They may be feelings of hurt, irritation, annoyance, or anger. Any feeling or description close to this will do. However, the ideas presented in this book so far may be so threatening that at first it's not necessary for people to *do* anything about the feelings; we just want them to be *aware* of what might be happening to them.

Often, I will ask a person like this to list five things that cause them some negative feelings during the upcoming week, and ask them to bring the list to their next session. Sometimes I have them carry a 3x5 card so they can record any feelings they have—negative or positive—during the week. Then we discuss the feelings and what they were related to. This assignment may be repeated for a number of weeks, until the person becomes more familiar with looking for the irritants in his life.

When the person becomes proficient in this step, I have him grade his feelings and what caused them to occur from a scale of one to ten. One stands for a very minimal injury, and ten for a maximum one.

Painstaking as it may be, this work is critical for the emotionally numb person to do. Such an individual is not only oblivious to negative feelings like anger, but to positive ones also, like joy, peace, and happiness.

The Overwhelmed Person

I worked with a woman who initially denied having any problem with anger. After a few weeks of listing her hurts she became amazed at how many things really did bother her. She then went to the other extreme of noting so many things that bothered her that she was overwhelmed by her feelings. First, I commended her for the excellent job she had done in getting in touch with her feelings. I then encouraged her to pick only one item that created a great deal of displeasure, and concentrate on applying the principles outlined in the previous chapters to resolve that problem. She could take a second or third item on a given week if she wanted to, but that was optional. If an item was too overwhelming to work on, an easier one could be substituted. In subsequent weeks, this procedure was repeated.

She was amazed to find that within a month several phenomenal things occurred. First, her suicidal depression was gone. Second, her feelings of worth skyrocketed; and third, her lists of hurts, irritations, and anger had greatly decreased. Last, her relationships improved markedly.

The Mismatched Couple

How do you help a couple when one partner is extremely proficient in dealing with conflict, and the other isn't? The proficient one is the type who is able to reason persuasively and "think on his feet." He might even slip into "the aggressor" role. The other partner struggles in these areas and is quickly overwhelmed when conflict arises. I frequently see this in my practice. When I see a couple like this I try to convey to them the idea that both individuals play a significant role in improving the situation. I liken it to a heavyweight boxer getting into the ring and teaching a novice bantamweight how to fight. Success will never be achieved unless the heavyweight deliberately restrains himself.

The partner who is more proficient in handling feelings and confronting must tone himself down in a conflict, especially avoiding any aggressiveness. There also must be tremendous sensitivity to the feelings of the one who is having the greater difficulty. There must be the awareness that if the more capable spouse keeps "winning" all the battles, both parties will ultimately lose. As the stronger one backs off and the other partner works on getting in touch and expressing his or her feelings, both will gain in the long run.

"I Don't Want to Hurt Anybody"

Colleen, a sensitive minister's wife, has been learning the principles of the preceding chapters. She now is in touch with feelings that were buried for years. Last week she was all set to start sharing some of her feelings with relatives and parishioners who have been taking her for granted. But she returned to the office this week stating that she couldn't share her feelings or confront anyone because she "didn't want to hurt anybody."

This is a frequent obstacle. Its roots usually go to the type of instructions a person may have received during his or her childhood. This person is often sensitive as to how confrontations might affect other people. When someone like Colleen expresses her feelings, she often finds that while the confrontation seems so strong, harsh, and uncomfortable to her, the other person hardly notices it. Colleen needs to be aware that the person she is confronting *may be* calloused, and she may need to be pretty strong to get through to them. It is true that if someone were to be that strong with her, she would probably be devastated. However, if she is speaking to someone who isn't as sensitive, she must come across pretty strong to even get his attention.

"I Blew It"

Sue finally mustered up enough courage to confront her neighbor about how she constantly used Sue as a baby sitter. Sometimes this friend just assumed that Sue would take care of her children. Sue had rehearsed in her mind how she would "constructively" approach her neighbor about the issue. Yesterday the neighbor brought her unruly two-year-old and simply stated, "I'll be back in two or three hours to pick him up." A surge of anger overwhelmed Sue and she blurted out, "You're always doing this; it makes me so angry."

Afterward, Sue sat in my office feeling very down and guilty for "attacking" her neighbor, and she retreated to her previous ways of burying all feelings. Her outburst had made her afraid she was becoming a hostile, aggressive person.

First of all, I commended Sue for trying to apply the principles of dealing with her frustration. It may be that she didn't apply them in the most ideal way, but for her this was a real step of progress. Then I drew for her something I share with patients who are having this problem. Illustration 8 shows a pendulum located in the center position. The center position I call "constructive" communication, while the right side is labeled "passive" communication and the left side "aggressive" communication.

Ideally, the pendulum should be centered. This is the optimum way to handle conflict. This is the way Sue should be handling her conflict with her neighbor.

This ideal way to handle conflicts is for a person to *constructively* communicate his appropriate needs, desires, and wishes. This should be done honestly and frankly without being aggressive. A person who communicates constructively is able to take a stand when needed, to express feelings, and to avoid mistreatment by others.

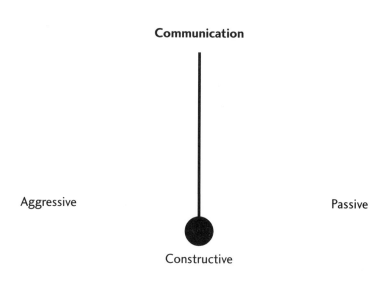

The Ideal Way
Illustration 8

One writer describes this type of communication as a vital interpersonal skill, an indicator of social competence, and a learned capability involving a complex repertoire of responses. He goes on to say that individuals without this skill "tend to be mistreated, fail to express feelings, and are frequently unable to have their needs met. A natural consequence of these problems is frustration and anger."[74]

Many individuals find themselves virtually immobilized as they try to appropriately express themselves. When they were young, a parent may have so injured them when they attempted to communicate their feelings that they gave up. Now it seems impossible for them to try to express their needs.

David Seamands tells a story of when he was a missionary to India. A vendor at a bazaar was selling a number of speckled brown quail. He had a string attached to one of the quail's legs, and the other end of the string was attached to a post. The quail kept walking around and around and around the post. A Brahman came by, a Hindu who believed in respect for all life, and said he would buy all the quail. When he had paid for them he told the merchant to cut the strings and let the quail loose. So the strings were cut off. But instead of flying away, they continued to march around and around the post. Finally the quail had to be shooed away to get them to fly off. But wherever they landed, they would walk in circles again.[75] They were free, but in a sense they were still bound. This graphically illustrates the plight of people I have seen who have been conditioned to bury all their feelings.

In one landmark experiment, a researcher put dogs in a cage and gave them a painful electrical shock. This caused them to express a lot of rage—they barked and howled, and tried to get out of the cage. But all their efforts were in vain. Eventually they gave up and lay on the floor of the cage, only to give a small yelp when they received another shock. Then the researchers removed one side of the cage so that the dogs could easily jump out and thus avoid the electrical shock. But guess what happened? Most of the dogs continued to stay on the floor of the cage and let out a faint yelp. This phenomenon came to be called *learned helplessness.*[76] Not infrequently I see this in patients. When they were growing up they were constantly put down. Some were even abused. They learned that they could do nothing about their feelings, so they stopped trying. Now, years later, they accept put-downs because of their early conditioning. It's difficult to get such a patient to risk expressing his or her feelings, needs, or desires. It's hard for such a person to really believe she can honestly and frankly communicate her hurts and that it will make a difference.

How does all of this fit in with Sue, who felt used by her neighbor as a baby sitter? When Sue was a child her alcoholic mother would rant and rave if she didn't comply with her mother's every wish. It's understandable that Sue has handled most conflict situations in a passive way ever since. Like the quail and dogs, during the early years of her life she couldn't escape abuse, and now as an adult she has been living as if she could not escape from people like her neighbor. She remains a perpetual victim. Sue's passive position is shown in Illustration 9 on the following page.

When Sue finally summoned the courage to confront her neighbor, she became angry and is convinced she "overreacted." Maybe her "blaming you" message to her neighbor was a little strong. She might have indeed over-swung into a slightly aggressive position, as shown in Illustration 10 on page 118.

In my opinion, this is better for Sue than staying passive and burying her feelings. I encouraged her to keep working at it. For her this was a positive step, even though she might have overreacted slightly. An overswing is sometimes a necessary step in the process of learning how to handle feelings appropriately.

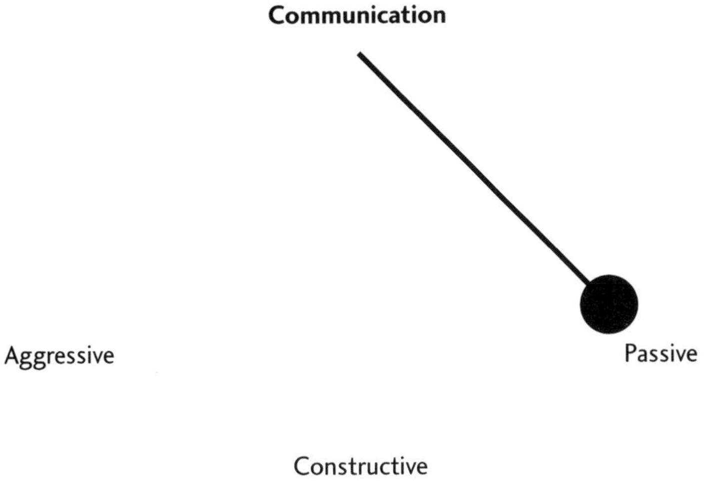

Communication

Aggressive   Passive

Constructive

The Passive Way
Illustration 9

Often people like Sue feel they are overreacting when they feel themselves swinging to the left, when in reality they are moving only slightly to the left. Their communication is still somewhat passive. This situation is pictured in Illustration 11 on page 119.

Let's return to Illustration 8. Ideally, the pendulum should be centered—this is our goal in handling conflict. In reality, no one except Christ can achieve this all the time. The best among us will veer slightly to the left or right from time to time, but most of the time we will practice fairly healthy communication. This center point should be Sue's ultimate goal in handling her conflicts.

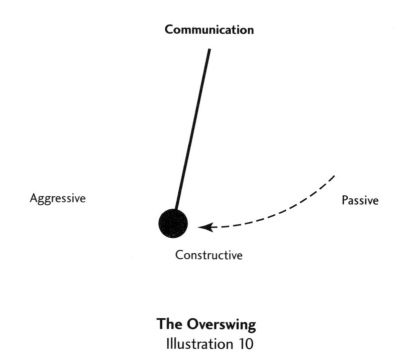

The Overswing
Illustration 10

With continued practice she will improve her skills, and in the meantime she should be satisfied with her honest efforts.

Dealing with Perpetual Put-Downs

One commonly expressed fear people have about confronting others or sending "I feel" messages is that they will either be laughed at or ignored. If you send an "I feel" message and someone laughs at you, I would suggest sending a second "I feel" message that expresses your feelings about being laughed at. You may even have to send

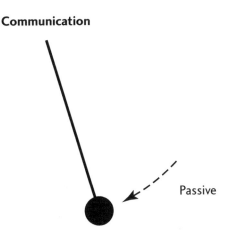

Communication

Aggressive   Passive

Constructive

The Non-Overswing
Illustration 11

two or more messages in succession before the person "hears" you.

A common means an aggressive person uses to control the more sensitive person is to put down his or her feelings. Let's say you have been in the habit of using "blaming you" messages. If you told your husband, "You're making me mad because you're paying so much attention to your secretary," your husband might retort with, "I'm not paying too much attention to her, I'm just doing my job—and besides, if you're mad, that's your problem." Clearly nothing was said that would help resolve the situation. But now let's say you used an "I feel" message instead, saying, "I'm feeling ignored." In doing so, you have decreased the likelihood of a negative response from your husband. When you don't make him feel threatened or defensive, he is more likely to say, "I'm sorry. I didn't mean to ignore you."

Unfortunately, many aggressive individuals are not likely to respond favorably to a constructive interaction because they would lose control. Many times I have had patients tell me that their spouse responded to constructive words with, "Oh, you're just too sensitive." If you stop at this point, you have gained nothing; in fact, overall it is a loss because you tried the "I feel" message and got put down in the process. A good response might be, "I don't think I'm too sensitive on this issue; however, I feel your sensitivity to my feelings is the real issue." Even after all this, a very controlling person will continue to fight for dominance. I would neither get into an argument with that person nor would I capitulate, in essence, saying, "You're right." Quietly but firmly hold to your position, remembering that you don't have to get in the last word.

"It Still Doesn't Work"

A few years ago in an adolescent psychotherapy group, a 16-year-old girl named Karen told about how her mother would go into her bedroom without knocking when she was undressing. This girl told the group that she shared her "I feel" messages once, twice, and three times without any success, but she kept on sending them. Later, she reported that "only after the twenty-seventh time did my mother get the message and change her behavior— but then it worked!"

Another way to handle an unresponsive person is with progressively stronger confrontations. The first time Karen's mother walked in her room without knocking, she could send a quiet "I feel" message such as, "It upsets me when you come into my room without knocking." If this did not improve the situation, Karen might say in a stronger but respectful voice, "Mother, do you know that I feel violated when you come into my room without knocking?"

If there is still no improvement on the mother's part, Karen could clearly show her feelings of anger and say, "*Mother,* I not only feel violated but hurt and angry when you continue to barge into my room when I am undressing. I'm also upset because you don't seem to value my feelings on this matter. Can we sit down and discuss this?" The next step might be to ask that Dad be included in the discussion. This process might need to continue to progress along these lines until the issue is resolved.

The principle that I am trying to illustrate is that if the other person doesn't respond to a soft "I feel" message, you may need to send progressively stronger messages.

When to Use These Principles

A question that frequently arises among those who have become acquainted with the steps outlined in chapters 7–8 is this: "How do I know if an issue should be dealt with according to these steps?" Generally, I advise that any issue or problem that is apt to keep crossing your mind with some feelings of hurt, irritation, or anger, especially for a day or more after the initial feelings of displeasure were noted, should be subjected to these steps. With the consistent application of these principles in your life, you will soon learn to recognize those issues which can be passed over immediately and those which may require further action.

Preventing Anger

If you want to be able to handle anger when it arises, then there is work that needs to be done during the times when you aren't angry. Your unresolved anger fund needs to be reduced of any balance that may have accumulated over your lifetime. Also, there are a number of things you need to evaluate in your life to ensure that you will respond maturely to conflict situations. Dealing with anger in the quiet periods when you're not angry will help to decrease the frequency, the intensity, and the inappropriateness of your anger.

Maintain a Purposeful Life

Good health habits are essential in minimizing anger. When we are tired we are much more prone to snap at others and to overreact to small irritants. Our tolerance for pressures and new problems is definitely lowered. Proper diet, rest, relaxation, and exercise are essential.

In addition to maintaining a physically active life, it is essential to maintain an active life in general. People who have positive pursuits in their lives have less time and reason to be angry than people who are stuck in a rut. The person who is progressing toward personal goals is less likely to be jealous of another person's success, which often manifests itself in anger. You need to have meaningful, constructive goals for both your work and your leisure hours.

Have a Proper Relationship with God

A right relationship with God is essential in giving a person a proper perspective on all the issues that we have been talking about. A right relationship with God also helps to eliminate the animosity that can arise between ourselves and others. When we remember all that God has done for us despite the hurts we have inflicted on others, it can't help but soften our tendency to be angry at others for the hurts that they have inflicted on us. In addition, regular time alone with God, reading the Bible, praying, and meditating on His Word can help clarify areas in our lives that need working on and can better prepare us to handle conflict in advance.

A compromised Christian life undoubtedly makes a person more prone to anger. The example of Balaam illustrates this (see Numbers 22:26-33). God allowed Balaam's donkey to irritate Balaam, which caused Balaam to pause in his wrongdoing. However, he got angry at his donkey and failed to see that it was God who was trying to warn him. When God needs to, in His permissive will, He can use disappointments, hurts, and suffering to get our attention. If we don't get the message, we may end up just getting angry. Job 36:18 says, "Don't let your anger at others lead you into scoffing at God! Don't let your suffering embitter you at the only one who can deliver you" (TLB).

Evaluate Your Rights and Expectations

Some people teach that we have no rights—that we should live to serve others and be willing to do whatever others ask of us, never thinking of our own desires or needs. They cite the passage in the Sermon on the Mount (Matthew 5–7) that tells us that if someone strikes us on the right cheek, we should offer the other cheek; that if someone asks us for our coat, we should give him our shirt also; that if someone forces us to walk a mile with him, we should go the second mile (Matthew 5:39-41). They see the Christian life as one of unquestioning submission, in which we take whatever comes our way and never offer any resistance. The implication of this teaching, in terms of anger, is that if we expect nothing from life or from others, we will not be disappointed and thus angry when we suffer misfortunes.

I believe it's normal to have certain rights and expectations. In fact, I would go so far as to say that if we really lived as if we had absolutely no rights we would be poor stewards of all that God has given us and would probably die in a short time. There are always people who have greater needs than ours, and if we believe we have no rights, we will give away everything we have and every shred of ourselves to these people who are more needy than we are. I agree that if we really believe we have no rights and do not have any expectations, much of our anger problem can be resolved. However, dealing with the *entire* problem of anger in this way is, in my opinion, very naïve.

On the other hand, there is no question that *inappropriate* rights and expectations are a major cause of problems for many people. People get angry if what they conclude to be their rights are not satisfied or if their expectations are not met. Very often these "rights" and expectations have never been fully put into words; in fact, they are sometimes subconscious or even unconscious in nature. And if those expectations were put into words, the person might be embarrassed or even deny them.

The more rights and expectations we claim, whether we are aware of them or not, the more things we have to get angry about. I have seen people in therapy who believe that society should take care of their needs, even though they are young and healthy. They would never admit this in so many words, but when you really get to know them it is clear that this is their expectation.

I can at the present moment think of several people who are angry over the fact that they have had to start at the bottom of the company and work up to the top. I know a wife who has concluded that it is her exclusive right to decide if her marriage is to remain intact. Then there are the husbands who act as if it is their exclusive right to decide 1) where the couple or family should take every vacation; 2) which car he should have (an expensive new car), and which car his wife should be happy with (an old inexpensive car); 3) how to control their finances. These are just a few of the rights and expectations that can create emotional havoc in interpersonal relationships.

Every time you get hurt, angry, frustrated, or disappointed, some contract that you hold onto is being violated.

You may protest, "I haven't entered into any contracts! What do you mean, some contract is being violated?" We all live within a myriad of contracts, many of which we are totally oblivious to. Every person in a close relationship—whether at home, at work, or within any other group—has at least three levels of expectations, which are listed below:

At the first level are the *expressed expectations*. These are the expectations that are clearly defined between you and the other person. They may be written or verbalized. At another level are the *unexpressed but conscious expectations*. These expectations are formulated in your mind, but you have never expressed them verbally. The reasons could be that you are uncomfortable disclosing what you actually expect of the other person, or you are afraid you might be rejected in some way.

Our expectations still don't stop at this level. There is one deeper level, the *unconscious expectations*, which are not clearly defined even to yourself.

In each close relationship, then (especially marriage), there are three levels of expectations that each individual has. This gives much opportunity for hurt, irritation, or anger to develop.[77]

There is a game often played in close relationships that I've called "The Hidden Test of Expectancy." It goes like this: The button is missing from my gray suit. I know my wife is aware of this because she happened to notice the button's absence the last time I wore the suit. I know she is busy, but a week has gone by and the button is still missing. I reason that *if she really loves me* she would have mended the suit without my having to bring it to her attention. *In fact,* I muse, *I'll just see how much she loves me by seeing how long it takes her to mend it.*

Another week passes, and one day she comments that I seem to be wearing my sports coat more frequently. I casually reply, "Well, I haven't worn it for a long time, so I thought I'd get a little wear out of it." However, as I drive to work, I realize that I'm irritated because she has failed my *hidden test of expectancy* by not sewing on the button yet.

It's not difficult to see how destructive this sort of game is. I believe that if we really care about a relationship, we need to work hard at stopping these games. When something is important to us, we must learn to share our *feelings and desires* with those of whom we have the expectations. The book *Caring Enough to Confront* says, "Keep short books with your feelings. Stay up to date. Find ways of reporting feelings as they occur. Experiment in saying both what you feel and what you really want."[78]

How can you determine if your expectations are realistic or not? Often the best way to find out is to list all the things that tend to upset you, irritate you, or make you angry. By taking a good hard look at each item on that list, you can usually figure out what kind of rights and expectations you feel entitled to.

There is no question in my mind that one of the quickest ways to change hurt and angry feelings is to look at your expectations and change those that are inappropriate or unrealistic. As those rights and expectations are changed, the anger will dissolve. On the other hand, if you don't deal with the inappropriate expectations, you will continue to react to other people with anger. I'm afraid that all too frequently we are afraid to be honest with ourselves about our expectations. We are often embarrassed to verbalize them even to ourselves, let alone to others. Nevertheless, our unconscious minds act on the basis of those expectations, whether we are fully aware of them or not. Thus it is crucial that we get in touch with our "rights" and "expectations" and evaluate their legitimacy.

Express Your Expectations

Once we have gotten in touch with all our expectations and have admitted them to ourselves, we need to express them to those of whom we have the expectations. That is the only way to have a truly honest, open relationship. Otherwise it's like two people trying to play a game when only one of them knows the rules. We need each other's feedback as to whether our expectations are valid and mutually agreed upon. Those that aren't mutually agreed upon must be negotiated, or else trouble will be inevitable.

In addition to expressing our expectations, we must also express our needs, and at times our wishes and desires. In close relationships like those at home, work, or church, so much hurt comes from failing to discuss these matters.

Many of us who want to be "nice" people cringe at the thought of expressing expectations. Somehow it doesn't seem that a loving person should do something as "uncaring" as this. However, I can assure you that withholding your desires will create more havoc than if you tactfully and honestly express them.

I know several Christians who accepted full-time Christian jobs, and when they entered into the negotiations about the job, they portrayed a "loving" and "anything's okay" attitude. But I have had the opportunity to keep in contact with some of these people for a number of years, and have since observed their nonverbalized and possibly unrealized expectations. When those expectations weren't met they were hurt, and sometimes even became angry and bitter. How much better it would have been for all the parties involved if they had honestly expressed their expectations at the beginning rather than allowing their frustrations to lead to the ill feelings that inevitably resulted.

Expect the Right Things from God

I believe that every person in this universe has expectations of God, regardless of his belief about the existence of God. One person says, "If God exists, He should be good and remove all evil and suffering from the earth." Another person may hold to the notion, "If there is a God, He should reveal Himself to me in a way that will not require faith on my part. He should prove Himself to me." Many people feel that they shouldn't have to suffer difficulties in life, whether physical, emotional, or financial. It's as though God owes them a comfortable life.

These expectations are seldom consciously thought through or verbalized, but they are nevertheless at work in daily life. To see this most vividly, observe the reactions of people who have lost a job, had a financial reversal, become seriously ill, or lost a loved one. The reactions that follow a disappointed expectation of God are often anger, resentment, bitterness, and depression.

What should we do if we find ourselves reacting negatively to our unmet expectations? Whether our expectations are appropriate or not, we need to be honest about all those feelings to ourselves and to God. This honesty with our feelings is healthy for several reasons:

Only as these expectations are put out in the open before God can they be dealt with effectively. People often ask, "Will God get angry if I express my negative feelings to Him?" The books of Psalms and Job are full of feelings of disappointment, misunderstanding, and anger being expressed to God. Jeremiah, Habakkuk, Job, and David all vented their pain and upset feelings, which probably helped them work through the difficult situations in which they found themselves. However, it is worthy to note that in venting our feelings and airing our doubts, questions, or fears to God—who already knows all about them—we must be careful not to curse God in the process (see Job 1:22).

Another reason that it is healthy to be honest about expectations is that only then are we in a position to sort out the appropriate ones from the inappropriate ones. For examples of people with inappropriate expectations in the Scriptures, see the accounts of Kings Ahab and Uzziah, who both became angry when their wishes were not met (1 Kings 21 and 2 Chronicles 26:16-20). Another example is the older brother who became angry when the prodigal son was honored by his father (Luke 15). In each case, expectations were not met, and anger was the result.

Job, although he was the most righteous man on the face of the earth at that time, had to give up his health, his prosperity, his family, and even his favor with his peers. This wasn't because he violated God's laws; it was because God had the right to allow those things to be taken from him. I realize that this may seem like an extreme example unrelated to life as many of us experience it today. However, if we just pick up a newspaper, we will see people who have lost everything through war, famine, earthquakes, or flooding.

We must continually be aware of what our expectations are and evaluate whether they are appropriate. We must be willing to give up any expectations that God desires to change. But let me hasten to make one more point: Sometimes after we have yielded something to God, He later restores it, giving even more in return. For example, Naaman wanted a pompous ceremony to cure his leprosy, but he had to give up that demand. When he followed the more humbling procedure of bathing in the muddy Jordan River, he was completely cured (2 Kings 5). Job surrendered his "rights" to health, wealth, and family, and later received back twice as much. As soon as these people were willing to yield their rights, God blessed them abundantly.

Accept the Facts of Life

When our only daughter was 21, she was diagnosed with acute leukemia. After chemotherapy failed, we were told she would die. For two years her life hung in the balance, but she was one of the fortunate ones because God intervened, and she is alive today. However, during the time that she battled with leukemia, we struggled with the feeling that life wasn't fair.

Many things in life don't seem to be fair. The person who is intelligent, successful, good-looking, healthy, and personable often has done nothing to get all these qualities. On the other extreme is the person with an average or low IQ and none of the qualities listed in the previous sentence. You and I are most likely somewhere between these two extremes. In the parable of the talents we read, "To one he gave five talents, to another, two, to another, one" (Matthew 25:15). Thus God Himself acknowledges the fact that individuals have various abilities.

If we compare ourselves with other people we will always seem to come out short. The Joneses will always seem to have more than we do. Even the person who has everything tends to ignore all that he has and instead focuses on what he doesn't have.

We need to see life more from God's perspective—that life is a gift. The years that we have are a gift. The degree of health, wealth, and wisdom we have are gifts. If we let ourselves envy others, we will miss the many things that God has done and is doing for us. Accepting ourselves and our assets—God's gifts to us—is fundamental to overcoming anger.

Be Realistic About Self-Expectations

Sometimes we expect too much of ourselves. We don't take into account—or we refuse to admit—that we are human and thus we have certain limitations. I have worked with patients who expected to get straight "A"s in college or graduate school, patients who demanded that their house always be immaculate, and patients who wanted to look like a model. This problem can express itself in the form of overextending ourselves, trying to cram too much into every minute of our lives. Then, when we can't accomplish what we set out to do, we become angry at ourselves or at whatever interferes with our schedule, such as a traffic jam or the fact that the toast burned.

Make a Contract

Expressing expectations and at times actually coming to a contractual agreement can save a great deal of time, money, and emotional energy. The Bible offers an example of such a contractual agreement: Abimelech and his men took possession of an important well that belonged to Abraham. Abraham diplomatically gave Abimelech a gift, and then obtained an agreement stating that the well was his (Genesis 21:25-32).

In my last year of residency in psychiatry I was allowed a certain amount of elective time to pursue special interests. I wanted to sharpen my skills in one particular area, but I had heard that this department tended to make increasingly more difficult demands on a person as time went on. I had observed some of the problems that this created for other residents. At first my choices seemed to be to either avoid this area altogether, which would have been to my loss, or else to allow myself to get involved, knowing that eventually I would become frustrated and angry when increasing demands were placed upon my already-busy schedule.

I didn't like either of these options, so I did something that, to my knowledge, no one had ever done before. I wrote a proposal that stated exactly what I wanted to do in the elective, the amount of time that I would be willing to give, and my expectations from the people involved. Furthermore, I listed a number of things that I did not want to see happen. Then I submitted the proposal to all the parties involved. Obviously, they had a free choice as to whether to accept my proposal, make changes to it, or reject it. As it turned out, they accepted the terms I had proposed.

Shortly afterward my superior kidded me, "Did you have a lawyer brother draft that contract?" I told him that I hadn't, but that I wanted to draft it for the sake of all involved and because of what I had observed happen to my colleagues in previous years. Despite this explanation, this same person put pressure on me three times to do more and more "for my *own* education." It was a great relief to me to be able to remind him of our mutual agreement and to suggest that we look at it together in case either of us had forgotten the items covered. He said, "No, that won't be necessary," and the pressure was removed.

If I had not drawn up that agreement, I probably would have been furious about the extra workload and had a difficult time resolving the conflict. However, with the contract in place, I was only slightly annoyed and was able to confront and then "pass over" the issue fairly easily without having it damage my relationship with the department or this individual. Clearly delineating one's expectations and perhaps even expressing them in the form of a contract can prevent a great deal of conflict.

Deal with Feelings of Inferiority

In my opinion there is a direct correlation between our feelings of inadequacy or inferiority and the anger in our lives. The more inadequate or inferior we feel, the greater the likelihood that we are going to be angry. On the other hand, the more we have a healthy appreciation for ourselves, the less reason we will have to be defensive, bitter, and jealous. (Notice, by the way, that I say our *feelings* of inadequacy and inferiority, because often there is very little correlation between our *feelings* of inadequacy and our *actual* capabilities. If we *feel* inadequate and inferior, we will be on our guard for anything that threatens our feelings of appropriate-worth, and so we are quick to protect ourselves with angry counterattacks.)

Avoid Aggravating Situations

"Do not associate with a man given to anger, or go with a hot-tempered man, lest you learn his ways, and find a snare for yourself" (Proverbs 22:24,25). We need to be aware that certain people are more prone to become angry, and that some of this anger may rub off on us. Also, certain situations may be more anger-producing than others, and unless we have an unusually good reason for being around these situations, we should consider removing ourselves.

Sometimes we find ourselves in situations where it is difficult to resolve anger constructively. An example might be the unreasonable boss. In such a circumstance we have to take a hard look at either changing ourselves or the relationship, and if neither of these is feasible, we may have to change jobs.

An unreasonable spouse is probably the most difficult situation in which we can find ourselves. Conscientiously applying the principles in this book can help tremendously, but when that is not enough, outside help is necessary. Other aggravating conditions include: A sweltering environment, changing weather conditions, clutter, excessive noise, and crowding.[79]

Socialization and Humor

Isolated individuals tend to have more trouble with unresolved anger, whereas individuals who have a good social network—significant relationships with others—tend to have less trouble with hurts and anger.[80]

Good humor has been shown to have positive health benefits.[81]

Teach Your Children How to Handle Hurts and Anger

It is now clear that patterns of expressing anger often begin in childhood and adolescence. Researchers have found children as young as seven who struggle with anger have an accompanying increase in their blood pressure.[82] Thus, it is crucial that parents and teachers model healthy ways to handle anger. Within the family, children need to see us handle anger appropriately. Hiding your anger at your spouse will not teach your children the skills they need in order to handle anger.

Reduce Your Unresolved Anger Fund

The amount of energy that is tied up in hurts and anger is truly incalculable. At a moment's notice King Herod's stepdaughter, after being advised by her mother, Herodias, rejected an offer of up to half the kingdom and instead chose to have John the Baptist beheaded. John had told King Herod that it wasn't lawful for him to be married to his brother's wife, Herodias. This angered Herodias, and so she "had a grudge against him and wanted to put him to death" (Mark 6:19). Like Herodias, many of us have large reserves in our unresolved anger fund which are using up tremendous amounts of emotional energy.

That brings us to this all-important question: How do we get rid of this unresolved anger fund? How do we deplete it? I think we can get answers by considering how this fund developed in the first place. Every time there was a situation that left a hurt or frustration that was not handled constructively, it accumulated in our unresolved anger fund. The charged emotions were pushed down inside. In order to get rid of this reserve in the anger fund, I believe we must go back and do the constructive work that was not done initially. This may seem to be a simplistic approach for dissipating destructive energy, but it is basically what must be done.

First, we must get in touch with the original feelings— the hurt, the pain, or the anger. The psychological term for the recall of repressed, painful memories and experiences is *abreaction*. Once a person has gotten in touch with his feelings, he then needs to handle them in a constructive way (as outlined in the previous chapters). Thus, if he has repressed the hurt and anger, he has only delayed doing the constructive work that must be done. And this person is paying a very high interest rate for every day he procrastinates in dealing constructively with that hurt or anger. Not only does he carry a tremendous weight around with him, but he may also be unable to achieve his maximum potential.

Someone might ask, "When a person becomes a Christian, aren't the old hurts in our lives removed? Aren't we the 'new creature' that 2 Corinthians 5:17 (KJV) talks about—'old things are passed away; behold, all things are become new'?" It is my opinion that when someone is converted, these things may or may not be resolved. That has nothing to do with whether the person is a Christian or is forgiven by God. If a person is born again he is a Christian and he is forgiven, but that doesn't necessarily mean that all the old hurts and wounds are automatically resolved.

I believe that some people are able to come to Christ after years of overt sin, and are able to immediately get in touch with their old buried hurts and anger. When they are saved, they actually get rid of most of their unresolved anger fund. Meanwhile, there are some who aren't as in touch with the old baggage and they may need to work on it at a later time. This has no effect on their salvation; they are still bound for heaven.

Then there are those who come to Christ at a young age before any kind of anger fund is built up. As the years pass, some of them accumulate a lot of unresolved hurt and anger. This could be due to factors such as poor role models, faulty instruction, naïve choices, or outright disobedience. Even though these people are Christians, they are weighed down. They may need help with getting in touch with their problems and associated feelings, and taking action.

When it comes to preventing anger in our lives, there is much we can do. This includes maintaining a purposeful life, having a right relationship with God, having realistic expectations, making contracts, avoiding feelings of inferiority, avoiding aggravating situations, socializing, and reducing our unresolved anger fund. In all these ways, we can diminish the impact of anger and enjoy more peaceful, enjoyable lives.

How to Communicate Constructively

Over the years I have found that many individuals and couples who get into trouble while communicating do so because they repeatedly violate some basic principles in communication. This greatly complicates their problems and increases the likelihood of developing anger, resentment, and bitterness. Therefore, I have developed some basic guidelines for cultivating constructive communication while in the midst of a conflict. I believe that 50 percent of the conflicts that couples have could be resolved by merely applying these principles.

1. *Never have any physical contact with your partner out of anger:* Even seemingly innocuous things like holding, pinching, or poking can escalate the conflict.

2. *Listen to your partner attentively:* Empathic listening—that is, putting yourself in the other person's position—is extremely helpful. Eye contact and body language is very important in communicating interest.

3. *"Share a meaning":* Often in arguments we are so concerned about our defense or what we are going to say next that we don't really hear what the other person has to say. If either party senses that this is happening, it's appropriate to ask for what's called a "shared meaning"—that is, for a restating of the issue. For instance, if you aren't really sure what the other person is trying to say, you might say, "I'd like to be sure that I understand what you're saying. Are you saying...?" Or, you might say to your partner, "I'm not sure we're on the same wavelength. Would you mind putting in your own words what I've just shared so that I can be sure that we are following each other?"

4. *Don't interrupt:* Make it a rule that whoever is speaking has the right to complete his or her thoughts without interruption. Both parties should try to speak fairly briefly and not, in essence, filibuster the situation. If this becomes a problem, you may have to agree on how much time each person is allowed to talk.

5. *Limit your discussion to only one issue:* If at all possible, stick to one subject. Many couples get into a great deal of trouble because, before long, they have a half a dozen different topics going, and when that occurs, nothing can be accomplished. If your partner pulls out a laundry list of gripes, keep the discussion focused on the original issue.

6. *Speak from your own perspective:* It is crucial that you speak from your own perspective and allow the other person the right to a differing view. Seldom, if ever, does either party have the absolute truth on a given issue. Two individuals witnessing the same automobile accident

often see it differently. Even if you fully believe you are in the right, if you state it in such a way as to give the other person some room, you are facilitating dialogue. For instance, instead of saying, "That is *not* what happened," instead say something like, "From my perspective it appears...."

7. *Use "I feel" messages and avoid "you" messages:* Typically, "you" messages feel attacking to the other party. Also, they seldom are defendable. On the other hand, if you speak about your own needs, wishes, wants, desires or viewpoint, you give the other person the right to be himself or herself and to have a differing perspective.

8. *Avoid put-downs:* A sweeping judgment or put-down is highly destructive. Statements such as, "You're stupid" or, "You can't do anything right" hinder constructive communication. You need to refrain from ridicule, shaming, judging, criticizing, and faultfinding. Devaluing body language such as eye-rolling, laughing, grimaces, or groans should be avoided.

9. *Avoid all-inclusive statements:* Avoid using words such as *never* or *always* when you make a point. To do so is to make sweeping generalizations, and typically what happens is that you end up arguing about whether or not the all-inclusive statement is true. Thus you have left the original discussion and are accomplishing nothing.

10. *Avoid humor during arguments:* Couples who are unable to resolve issues very well usually find humor or sarcasm to be highly destructive. Unless your relationship is strong and secure, avoid using humor during arguments.

11. *Avoid assumptive mind-reading:* Sometimes one partner assumes the other person knows or should know what he or she is thinking. Or the reverse can be true: You might guess at what the other party is thinking without checking it out. Either way, assumptions usually lead to trouble.

12. *Try not to be the "authority":* There is often a temptation for at least one party to come across as the authority. This can take two forms: parenting and patronizing. Parenting statements include ordering, directing, admonishing, threatening, moralizing, preaching, advising, giving solutions, using logic, interpreting, analyzing, diagnosing, probing, questioning, or interrogating. Patronizing statements take the form of excessive or inappropriate reassuring, sympathizing, or consoling. All these are destructive for adult-to-adult communication.

13. *Continue the dialogue until both parties have said all that they want to say:* Storming out of a conversation or using the silent treatment are highly destructive. However, do not continue the dialogue when any of the following situations occur:

- If a person is unable to collect his or her thoughts on the issue and needs some time to think it through.

- If either party feels like he or she might lose control physically. Both of these are reasons to stop the discussion and possibly separate for a time. However, as soon as it is feasible, the dialogue should be continued, and it's the responsibility of the person who stopped the discussion to initiate further conversation.

• If the timing is inappropriate; for example, if you have to leave to pick up the kids from school, or it's 2:00 A.M. and one or both of you has to get up at 6:00 A.M. In such cases it is usually best to recess until a better, mutually agreed upon time to pick up the conversation.

A final note: When one person violates these guidelines I urge the other party not to make an issue of it and, if possible, not to even mention it. I recommend that they simply continue on with the dialogue and continue practicing the guidelines to the best of their ability.

Ultimately, the goals to achieve in constructive communication are as follows: 1) To understand each other clearly and to have both parties feel "heard." Many conflicts can be resolved if this goal alone is reached. 2) To brainstorm on possible solutions to deal with the differences. 3) To agree on a final solution. Sometimes this will be a compromise between the two positions; at other times the solution may be in accordance with one party's wishes and at other times the other party's wishes. 4) A trial period to implement the solution. 5) To agree to drop the issue so that it does not continue to extract an emotional price tag on the relationship. 6) And finally, to resolve all ill feelings, remove any walls in the relationship, and to be fully reconciled, or, in a marriage, "to kiss and make up."

It is my opinion and experience that a significant percent of arguments, hurts, and anger could be avoided if these guidelines are followed. Even if only one person follows these guidelines, the dialogue will be significantly improved.

Handling Anger in a Christlike Way

Our ultimate goal should be to handle anger-producing situations in the most mature way possible—in a Christlike way. When it came to handling anger, Christ excelled in five important areas: 1) His ability to stand up for righteous principles; 2) His ability to pass over inconsequential issues; 3) His ability to forgive; 4) His willingness to pray for those who hurt Him; 5) His ability to love despite all that was done to Him.

In my opinion, we should endeavor to excel in all five areas from a position of strength, not weakness. We must be able to do all the things that have been listed earlier in this book to resolve anger, and only choose these more difficult means in certain situations. For example, I don't think you can truly pass over an issue, love, or forgive if you aren't able and willing to confront the person. You may decide to pass over the issue, but not because you are afraid of confronting the person.

A person must be emotionally and spiritually mature to apply these more difficult methods. He must genuinely care about the relationship. He must feel secure and loved by God. His deepest aim must be to please Christ.

If you found it difficult to use some of the constructive means described earlier in this book, I suggest that you work on those more, before you work on these more difficult methods.

Stand for Righteous Principles

Christian leaders down through centuries have described God's anger as "righteous indignation." However, I think the expression should be changed to *standing for righteous principles*. Christ's entire life was given to this goal, and at times while He was standing for righteous principles, it became necessary for Him to express anger.

Sometimes, you'll find a religious person who cloaks his anger in otherwise good religious or moral enterprise. However, God knows the true purpose of the heart, and if our motives aren't pure, our righteous indignation is actually *selfish* indignation.

The most obvious example of when Christ stood up for righteous principles is when He threw the money changers out of the temple because they were desecrating it (John 2:13-17). There were also other times that He expressed anger, especially towards the religious leaders of the day, whose legalism and hypocrisy hindered the common man from knowing God. In addition, many godly men throughout the Scriptures stood for righteous principles, such as Moses, Jonathan, Jeremiah, and Paul (see Exodus 19; 1 Samuel 19,20; Jeremiah 6:11; Acts 13:9-11).

Pass Over Inconsequential Issues

Christ had the ability to pass over inconsequential issues; that is, issues where no righteous principles were at stake. We discussed earlier how the crowd laughed at Jesus for saying Jairus' daughter was not dead but sleeping. After that He raised her from the dead, and resisted the temptation to tell the crowd, "I told you so."

I have chosen to use the phrase "pass over inconsequential issues" because I think it helps clarify an important distinction. When we aren't very mature, a personal attack may be of major consequence to us and there may be times when we will need to defend ourselves. However, as we feel better about ourselves both emotionally and spiritually, we will feel less and less need to defend ourselves because the issue will actually have become less important to us. In addition, as we are able to deal more constructively with the hurts and anger in our lives, our sense of worth will improve so that we will be able to pass over more and more issues. Proverbs 19:11 says, "A wise man restrains his anger and overlooks insults. This is to his credit" (TLB).

As we grow, eventually we will be in a position to choose to pass over more issues because they will become more inconsequential to us. It is out of strength that we are able to pass over these things. Christ was sure of His position with God, and the more sure we are of our own position with God, the more inconsequential certain issues will be.

At the same time, we cannot always expect this level of emotional and spiritual maturity from others. We must be cautious about expecting others to pass over issues which are crucial to them. I believe we have to be very careful about telling a five-year-old to "turn the other cheek." When other people hurt him, it is of major consequence to him. He may have to deal with it as most other five-year-olds do.

Forgive

Before we look at Jesus' ability and willingness to forgive, let's take a look at God's forgiveness toward us. First, it is the ultimate example of the kind of forgiveness that we should aim for, and second, as we become aware of how much God has forgiven us, it truly tends to eclipse the wrongs others have inflicted on us.

God promises not only to forgive our sins, but to forget them. He chooses not to remember them anymore. In Isaiah 38:17 we read, "Thou hast cast all my sins behind thy back" (KJV), and in Isaiah 43:25 God says, "I, even I, am the one who wipes out your transgressions for My own sake; and I will not remember your sins." The Living Bible renders this verse, "I, yes, I alone am he who blots away your sins for my own sake and will never think of them again." In Hebrews 8:12 the Lord says, "I will be merciful to their iniquities, and I will remember their sins no more."

Christ is our example of this kind of forgiveness. Although He was equal with God, He gave up His rights and took upon Himself the status of a slave, and was obedient even to the point of death (Philippians 2:5-8). Jesus took upon Himself the death penalty for our sins so that we could be forgiven. The Gospels record how the crowds made fun of Him, mocked Him, and humiliated Him; the soldiers stripped Him, beat Him, spit on Him, and finally hung Him on a cross to die a slow and painful death. And what was His response to all of this? "Father, forgive them; for they do not know what they are doing" (Luke 23:34).

You might say, "These altruistic examples are great, but what about the rest of us? We're not perfect like Christ." Stephen is a beautiful example of a young man who followed Jesus' example (Acts 7). After he had shared the gospel with those around him, he was rejected along with the message he was trying to give. He knew he was right and his audience was wrong, but to him, that wasn't the issue. Even while they were stoning him, he fell to his knees and cried out with a loud voice, "Lord, do not hold this sin against them!" (Acts 7:59,60).

In Matthew 18 we are told that if someone wrongs us, we are to confront him or her privately. If that doesn't resolve the problem, then we may have to involve others. However, immediately following such confrontation, we are told to forgive the person.

Peter once asked Christ how many times a man should forgive his brother. Peter thought seven times was generous. But Jesus' answer was "seventy times seven" or 490 times, thus suggesting that our forgiveness should be virtually limitless (Matthew 18:21,22). Christ then illustrated this point by telling of a man who owed twenty million dollars to the king, but the king forgave him the debt. Then the man who had just been forgiven viciously demanded repayment from a poor man who owed him only 20 dollars.

When the king heard this, he told the forgiven man, "'You evil-hearted wretch! Here I forgave you all that tremendous debt, just because you asked me to—shouldn't you have mercy on others, just as I had mercy on you?' Then the angry king sent the man to the torture chamber until he had paid every last penny due. So shall my heavenly Father do to you if you refuse to truly forgive your brothers" (Matthew 18:32-34 TLB).

As you can see, when we become fully aware of the magnitude of our sins and God's immeasurable forgiveness to us, any wrongs that others have committed against us suddenly look trivial.

The Lord's Prayer also emphasizes this principle of forgiveness. It says, in part, "Forgive us our sins, *just as we have forgiven those who have sinned against us....* Your heavenly Father will forgive you if you forgive those who sin against you; but if you refuse to forgive them, he will not forgive you" (Matthew 6:12-15 TLB, emphasis added, see also Mark 11:25).

We see this principle further exemplified in the books of 1 and 2 Corinthians. In 1 Corinthians 5, Paul told the church at Corinth to confront one of its members and take disciplinary action against him. Later, in 2 Corinthians, he wrote, "Now it is time to forgive him and comfort him. Otherwise he may become so bitter and discouraged that he won't be able to recover. Please show him now that you still do love him very much.... A further reason for forgiveness is to keep from being outsmarted by Satan; for we know what he is trying to do" (2 Corinthians 2:7,8,11 TLB).

Forgiveness means giving up a right. It means that you cancel a debt that someone owes you; it is costly. When we forgive, we suffer a loss ourselves. If we don't forgive, we are adamantly holding on to our "rights" and are continuing to demand some sort of psychological "payment" from the other person, even though it may be impossible for him to undo the wrong he has committed against us. If we are harboring anger or hurt, we are retaining our right for vengeance. We need to realize that forgiveness is largely a matter of the will. As Archibald Hart says, "Forgiveness is surrendering my right to hurt you back if you hurt me."[83]

In addition, I believe that there is a relationship between how forgiven we feel and how readily we forgive others. When a person doesn't forgive others, he labors under a tremendous amount of guilt and a feeling of not being fully forgiven. It is almost a case of misery loving company—if you feel miserable and guilty, so why shouldn't someone else feel that way too?

Following the verse that has been quoted many times in this book—"Be angry, and yet do not sin"—is the following admonition: "Let all bitterness and wrath and anger and clamor and slander be put away from you, along with all malice. And be kind to one another, tenderhearted, *forgiving each other,* just as God in Christ also has forgiven you" (Ephesians 4:31,32, emphasis added).

Pray for the Offender

Christ's love was so great that He was even able to pray for those who crucified Him. In this, He has given us an example to follow.

Job's friends, though they intended to help him, actually hurt him. The fact that they hurt him displeased God. Furthermore, God required Job to pray for his friends. When he did, the friends received forgiveness. This act of praying for them opened the door so that God could restore all that had been taken from Job; in fact, twice as much as he had before.

Be Loving

The very essence of the Bible is God's willingness to love us despite all our sin. The Bible says, "God so loved the world" that He was able to give His most precious possession, His Son (see John 3:16). He was willing not only to forgive but to love.

In 1 John 4:19 we read, "We love, because He first loved us." Romans 12:17-21 says, "Never pay back evil for evil to anyone.... If possible, so far as it depends on you, be at peace with all men. Never take your own revenge.... But if your enemy is hungry, feed him, and if he is thirsty, give him a drink; for in so doing you will heap burning coals upon his head. Do not be overcome by evil, but overcome evil with good."

Christ is our example of One who was willing to love even those who wronged Him, hurt Him, betrayed Him, rejected Him, deserted Him, beat Him, and in the end killed Him. As we come to understand His great love and forgiveness toward us, it will empower us to forgive and love those who hurt and wrong us in our day-to-day lives.

Notes

Chapter 1—Misconceptions About Anger

1. Joseph R. Cooke, *Free for the Taking,* Fleming H. Revell, Old Tappan, NJ, 1975, pp. 109-110.

Chapter 2—Camouflaging Anger

2. James Alsdurf & Phyllis Alsdurf, *Battered into Submission: The Tragedy of Wife Abuse in the Christian Home,* InterVarsity Press, Downers Grove, IL, 1989.

Chapter 3—The Catastrophic Results of Mishandled Anger

3. Early definitions of Type A behavior described behavior such as: excessive drive, competitive, achievement-oriented, a sense of time urgency, involved in multiple activities with deadlines, impatience, unrealistic ambition, and the need for control, impatient with slowness in others, rapid work pace, and tendency to be hostile. More current literature is focusing more on the role of anger, hostility, and aggression.

4. See Redford B. Williams, "Psychologic Factors in Coronary Artery Disease: Epidemiological Evidence," *Circulation,* 1987, Vol. 76 (suppl I), pp. I-117-I-123; Richard L. Verrier, Ph.D., and Murray A. Mittleman, M.D., Dr.P.H., "Life-Threatening Cardiovascular Consequences of Anger in Patient with Coronary Heart Disease," *Cardiology Clinics,* May 1996, Vol. 14, No. 2, pp. 289-307; Murray A. Mittleman, et al., "Triggering of Acute Myocardia Infarction Onset by Episodes of Anger," *Circulation,* 1995, Vol. 92, pp. 1720-1725.

5. Charles D. Spielberger, et al., "The Experience and Expression of Anger: Construction and Validation of an Anger Expression Scale" in *Anger and Hostility in Cardiovascular and Behavioral Disorders,* ed. Margaret A. Chesney, Ph.D. and Ray H. Rosenman, M.D., Hemisphere Publishing Corporation, WA, 1985, pp. 5-28.

6. See John C. Barefoot, et al., "Hostility, CHD Incidence and Total Mortality: A 25-year Follow-Up Study of 255 Physicans," *Psychosomatic Medicine,* 1983, Vol. 45, No. 1, pp. 59-63; Gail Ironson, et al., "Effects of Anger on Left Ventricular Ejection Fraction in Coronary Artery Disease," *American Journal of Cardiology,* 1992, Vol, 70, pp. 281-285; Karen A. Matthews, "Coronary Heart Disease and Type A Behaviors: Update on and Alternative to the Booth-Kewley and Friedman (1987) Quantitative Review," *Psychological Bulletin,* 1988, Vol. 14, No. 3, pp. 373-380; Michael F. Scheir, Ph.D., and Michael W. Bridges, M.S., "Person

Variables and Health: Personality Predispositions and Acute Psychological States as Shared Determinants for Disease" (Review), *Psychosomatic Medicine,* 1995, Vol. 57, No. 3, pp. 255-268; Richard B. Shekelle, et al., "Hostility, Risk of Coronary Heart Disease, and Mortality," *Psychosomatic Medicine,* 1983, Vol. 45, No. 2, pp. 109-114; Edward C. Suarez & Redford B. Williams, Jr., "Situational Determinants of Cardiovascular and Emotional Reactivity in High and Low Hostile Men," *Psychosomatic Medicine,* 1989, Vol. 51, pp. 404-418.

7. Richard L. Verrier, Ph.D., and Murray A. Mittelman, M.D., Ph.D., "Cardiovascular Consequences of Anger and Other Stress States," *Baillieres Clinical Neurology,* July 1997, Vol. 6, No. 2, pp. 245-259.

8. Murray A. Mittleman, et al., "Triggering of Acute Myocardial Infarction Onset by Episodes of Anger," *Circulation,* 1995, Vol. 92, pp. 1720-1725.

9. Peter Reich, et al., "Acute Psychological Disturbances Preceding Life-Threatening Ventricular Arrhythmias," *JAMA,* 1981, Vol. 246, pp. 233-235.

10. See Paul Hjemdahl, M.D., et al., "Effects of Stress and Beta-Blockade on Platelet Function," *Circulation,* 1991, Vol. 84 [suppl. VI], pp. VI-44-VI-61; Christina Jern, et al., "Changes of Plasma Coagulation and Fibrinolysis in Response to Mental Stress," *Thrombosis and Haemostasis,* 1989, Vol. 62, No. 2, pp. 767-771; Shirley P. Levine, et al., "Platelet activation and secretion associated with emotional stress," *Circulation,* 1985, Vol. 71, No. 6, pp. 1129-1134.

11. See Jo Anne Grunbaum, et al., "The Association Between Anger and Hostility and Risk Factors for Coronary Heart Disease in Children and Adolescents: a Review," *Annuals of Behavior Medicine,* 1997, Vol. 19, No. 2, pp. 179-189; Redford B. Williams, Jr., *The Trusting Heart,* Random House, New York, 1989, pp. 23, 107.

12. Alan C. Yeung, et al., "The Effect of Atherosclerosis on the Vasomotor Response of Coronary Arteries to Mental Stress," *New England Journal of Medicine,* 1991, Vol. 325, pp. 1551-1556.

13. Michael D. Boltwood, Ph.D., et al., "Anger Report Predicts Coronary Artery Vasomotor Response to Mental Stress in Atherosclerotic Segments," *American Journal of Cardiology,* 1993, Vol. 72, pp. 1361-1365.

14. Alan C. Yeung, et al., "The Effect of Atherosclerosis on the Vasomotor Response of Coronary Arteries to Mental Stress," *New England Journal of Medicine,* 1991, Vol. 325, pp. 1551-1556.

15. See Gail Ironson, et al., "Effects of Anger on Left Ventricular Ejection Fraction in Coronary Artery Disease," *American Journal of Cardiology,* 1992, Vol. 70, pp. 281-285; Frances H. Gabbay, et al., "Triggers of Myocardial Ischemia During Daily Life in Patients with Coronary Artery Disease: Physical Mental Activities, Anger and Smoking," *Journal of American College of Cardiology,* 1996, Vol. 27, pp. 585-592.

16. John C. Barefoot, et al., "Hostility, CHD Incidence and Total Mortality: A 25-Year Follow-Up Study of 255 Physicians," *Psychosomatic Medicine*, 1983, Vol. 45, No. 1, pp. 59-63.

17. Ichiro Kawachi, et al., "A Prospective Study of Anger and Coronary Heart Disease; The Normative Aging Study," *Circulation*, 1996, Vol. 94, pp. 2090-2095.

18. See W. Doyle Gentry, et al., "Habitual Anger-Coping Styles: I. Effect on Mean Blood Pressure and Risk for Essential Hypertension," *Psychosomatic Medicine*, May 1982, Vol. 44, No. 2, pp. 195-201; Erick L. Diamond, "The Role of Anger and Hostility in Essential Hypertension and Coronary Heart Disease," *Psychological Bulletin,*1982, Vol. 92, No. 2, pp. 410-433; Charles Pernini, et al., "Suppressed Aggression and Hyperdynamic Cardiovascular Regulation in Normotensives Offspring of Essential Hypertensive Patients, *Journal of Cardiovascular Pharmacology,* 1988, Vol. 12 (Suppl. 3), pp. S130-S133.

19. See Kevin T. Larkin and Claudia Zayfert, "Anger Management Training with Mild Essential Hypertensive Patients," *Journal of Behavioral Medicine,* 1996, Vol. 19, No. 5, pp. 415-433; John Sommers-Flanagen, Ph.D., and Roger P. Greenberg, Ph.D., "Psychosocial Variables and Hypertension: A New Look at an Old Controversy," *Journal of Nervous and Mental Disease*, 1989, Vol. 177, No. 1, pp. 15-24.

20. W. Doyle Gentry, et al., "Habitual Anger-Coping Styles: I. Effect on Mean Blood Pressure and Risk for Essential Hypertension," *Psychosomatic Medicine*, May 1982, Vol. 44, No. 2, pp. 195-201.

21. See W. Doyle Gentry, Ph.D., *Anger Free: Ten Basic Steps to Managing Your Anger*, William Morrow and Company, Inc., New York, NY, 1999, p. 62; D. T. Gianturco, et al., "Personality Patterns and Life Stress in Ischemic Cerebrovascular Disease, 1. Psychiatric Findings," *Stroke*, 1994, Vol. 5, pp. 453-460.

22. Yoshitaro Matsumoto, et al., "Do Anger and Aggression Affect Carotid Atherosclerosis?" *Stroke,* 1993, Vol. 24, pp. 983-986.

23. Christina Jern, et al., "Changes of Plasma Coagulation and Fibrinolysis in Response to Mental Stress," *Thrombosis and Haemostasis,* 1989, Vol. 62, No. 2, pp. 767-771.

24. James W. Pennebaker, et al., "Disclosure of Traumas and Immune Function: Health Implications for Psychotherapy," *Journal of Consulting and Clinical Psychology,* 1988, Vol. 56, No. 2, pp. 139-245.

25. Michael F. Scheir, Ph.D., and Michael W. Bridges, M.S., "Person Variables and Health: Personality Predispositions and Acute Psychological States as Shared Determinants for Disease (Review)," *Psychosomatic Medicine*, 1995, Vol. 57, No. 3, pp. 255-268; Richard B. Shekelle, et al., "Hostility, Risk of Coronary Heart Disease, and Mortality," *Psychosomatic Medicine,* 1983, Vol. 45, No. 2, pp. 109-114; Redford Williams, M.D. and Virginia Williams, Ph.D., *Anger Kills: 17 Strategies*

for Controlling the Hostility that Can Harm Your Health, Harper Paperbacks, NY, 1998.

26. John C. Barefoot, et al., "Hostility, CHD Incidence and Total Mortality: A 25-Year Follow-Up Study of 255 Physicians," *Psychosomatic Medicine,* 1983, Vol. 45, No. 1, pp. 59-63.

27. Redford Williams, M.D. and Virginia Williams, Ph.D., *Anger Kills: 17 Strategies for Controlling the Hostility that Can Harm Your Health,* Harper Paperbacks, NY 1998, p. 3.

28. S. R. Wenneberg, et al., "Anger Expression Correlates with Platelet Aggregation," *Behavioral Medicine,* Winter 1997, Vol. 22, No. 4, pp. 174-177; Ernest Harburg, Ph.D., et al., "Resentful and Reflective Coping with Arbitrary Authority and Blood Pressure: Detroit," *Psychosomatic Medicine,* May 1997, Vol. 41, No. 3, pp. 189-202; William T. Riley, et al., "Anger and Hostility in Depression," *Journal of Nervous and Mental Disease,* 1989, Vol.177, No. 11, pp. 668-674.

29. Ichiro Kawachi, et al., "A Prospective Study of Anger and Coronary Heart Disease; The Normative Aging Study," *Circulation,* 1996, Vol. 94, pp. 2090-2095.

30. Redford Williams, M.D. and Virginia Williams, Ph.D., *Anger Kills: 17 Strategies for Controlling the Hostility that Can Harm Your Health,* Harper Paperbacks, NY, 1998, p. 60.

31. Theodore Isaac Rubin, *The Angry Book,* London, The MacMillan Company, 1969. Dr. Rubin, on page 24, refers to this as the "slush fund."

32. James W. Pennebaker, et al., "Disclosure of Traumas and Immune Function: Health Implications for Psychotherapy," *Journal of Consulting and Clinical Psychology,* 1988, Vol. 56, No. 2, pp. 139-245.

33. Karin F. Helmers, et al., "Defensive Hostility: Relationship to Multiple Markers of Cardiac Ischemia in Patients with Coronary Disease," *Health Psychology,* 1995, Vol. 14, No. 3, pp. 202-209.

34. Margaret A. Chesney, Ph.D. and Ray H. Rosenman, M.D., eds. *Anger and Hostility in Cardiovascular and Behavioral Disorders,* Hemisphere Publishing Corporation, WA, 1985, pp. 104-106, 150-151; Harold A. Kahn, et al., "The Incidence of Hypertension and Associated Factors: The Israel Ischemic Heart Disease Study," *American Heart Journal,* 1972, Vol. 84, No. 2, pp. 171-181; Charles Pernini, et al., "Suppressed Aggression and Hyperdynamic Cardiovascular Regulation in Normotensives Offspring of Essential Hypertensive Patients," *Journal of Cardiovascular Pharmacology,* 1988, Vol. 12 (Suppl 3), pp. S130-S133.

35. Ernest Harburg, Ph.D., et al., "Resentful and Reflective Coping with Arbitrary Authority and Blood Pressure: Detroit," *Psychosomatic Medicine,* May 1997, Vol. 41, No. 3, pp. 189-202.

36. Harris S. Goldstein, et al., "Relationship of Resting Blood Pressure and Heart Rate to Experienced Anger and Expressed Anger," *Psychosomatic Medicine*, 1988, Vol. 50, pp. 321-329.

37. Margaret A. Chesney, Ph.D. and Ray H. Rosenman, M.D., eds., *Anger and Hostility in Cardiovascular and Behavioral Disorders*, Hemisphere Publishing Corporation, Washington, 1985, p. 150.

38. See Jerome H. Markovitz, M.D., et al., "Psychological Predictors of Hypertension in the Framingham Study: Is There Tension in Hypertension?" *JAMA*, Nov. 24, 1993, Vol. 270, No. 20, pp. 2439-2443; Charles Pernini, et al., "Psychosomatic Factors in Borderline Hypertensive Subjects and Offspring of Hypertensive Patients," *Hypertension*, 1990, Vol. 16, pp. 627-634.

39. See Howard S. Friedman, and Stephanie Booth-Kewley, "Personality, Type A Behavior, and Coronary Heart Disease: The Role of Emotional Expression," *Journal of Personality and Social Psychology*, 1987, Vol. 53, No. 4, pp. 783-792; Suzanne G. Haynes, et. al., "The Relationship of Psychosocial Factors to Coronary Heart Disease in the Framingham Study: III. Eight Year Incidence of Coronary Heart Disease," *American Journal of Epidemiology*, 1980, Vol. 111, No.1, pp. 37-58.

40. See Eugenia W. Becker and Walter J. Lesiak, "Feelings of Hostility and Personal Control as Related to Depression," *Journal of Clinical Psychology*, 1977, Vol. 33, No. 3, pp. 654-657; Suman J. M. Fernando, "Hostility, Personality and Depression," *British Journal of Medical Psychology*, 1977, Vol. 50, pp. 243-249; Lee Goldman, Ph.D., and David A. Haaga, Ph.D., "Depression and the Experience and Expression of Anger in Marital and Other Relationships," *Journal of Nervous Mental Disease*, 1995, Vol. 183, pp. 505-509.

41. Terry W. Moore and Joseph G. P. Paolillo, "Depression: Influence of Hopelessness, Locus of Control, Hostility, and Length of Treatment," *Psychological Reports*, 1982, Vol. 54, pp. 875-881.

42. See Gabriel A. Kune, et al., "Personality as a Risk Factor in Large Bowel Cancer: Data from the Melbourne Colorectal Cancer Study," *Psychological Medicine*, 1991, Vol. 21, pp. 29-41; S. Greer and Tina Morris, "Psychological Attributes of Women Who Develop Breast Cancer: A Controlled Study," *Journal of Psychosomatic Research*, 1975, Vol. 19, pp. 147-153; Lydia Temoshock, et al., "The Relationship of Psychosocial Factors to Prognostic Indicators in Cutaneous Malignant Melanoma," *Journal of Psychosomatic Research*, 1985, Vol. 29, pp. 135-153.

43. See Harold L. Levitan, M.D., "Psychological Factors in the Etiology of Ulcerative Colitis: Objectlessness and Rage," *International Journal Psychiatry in Medicine*, 1976-77, Vol. 7, No. 3, pp. 221-228; Elliot N. Gale, "Psychological Characteristics of Long-Term Female Temporomandibular Joint Pain Patients," *Journal of Dental Research*, March 1978, Vol. 57, No. 3, pp. 481-483; W. Doyle

Gentry, Ph.D., *Anger Free: Ten Basic Steps to Managing Your Anger*, William Morrow and Company, Inc, New York, N.Y., 1999, pp. 12, 29, 61, 62; Jane Middelton-Moz, *Boiling Point: The High Cost of Unhealthy Anger to Individuals and Society*, Health Communications, Inc., Deerfield Beach, Florida, 1999, p. 32.

44. Larry Arnold, et al., "The Man Who Became Angry Once: A Study of Over Controlled Hostility," *Canadian Journal of Psychiatry*, 1979, Vol. 24, pp. 762-766.

45. Howard Kassinove, Ph.D., ABPP, (editor), *Anger Disorders: Definition, Diagnosis, and Treatment*, Taylor & Francis, Publishers, Washington, D.C., 1995, p. 28.

Chapter 4—Biblical Principles About Anger

46. W. E. Vine, *Expository Dictionary of New Testament Words* (Volume III), Fleming H. Revell, Co., Old Tappan, NJ, Seventeenth Impression, 1966, p. 93.

47. Kenneth S. Wuest, *Word Studies from the Greek New Testament*, Eerdmans Publishing Company, 1994, p. 114.

Chapter 5—How Do You Handle Your Anger?

48. Simon Kemp and K. T. Strongman, "Anger Theory and Management: A Historical Analysis," *American Journal of Psychology*, 1995, Vol. 108, No. 3, pp. 397-417.

49. R. W. Smith, "Hostility and Health: Current Status of a Psychosomatic Hypotheses." *Health Psychology*, 1992, Vol. 11, No. 3, pp. 139-150.

50. Margaret A. Chesney, Ph.D. and Ray H. Rosenman, M.D., eds. *Anger and Hostility in Cardiovascular and Behavioral Disorders*, Hemisphere Publishing Corporation, Washington, 1985, pp. 1-2; Christopher I. Eckhardt, et al., "Anger and Hostility in Maritally Violent Men: Conceptual Distinctions, Measurement Issues, and Literature Review," *Clinical Psychology Review*, 1997, Vol. 17, No. 4, pp. 333-358.

51. W. Doyle Gentry, Ph.D., *Anger Free: Ten Basic Steps to Managing your Anger*, William Morrow and Company, Inc., New York, N.Y., 1999, p. 14.

52. The diagram has been adapted from the Johari Window, first described by Luft and Ingham in 1955 and described by Joseph Luft in *Group Processes: An Introduction to Group Dynamics*, published by Mayfield Publishing Company, copyright 1963, 1970. Used by permission.

Chapter 6—Preparing to Handle Anger

53. David Mace, *Love and Anger in Marriage*, Grand Rapids, MI, Zondervan, 1982, as quoted in Redford Williams, M.D. and Virginia Williams, Ph.D., *Anger Kills: 17 Strategies for Controlling the Hostility that Can Harm Your Health*, Harper Paperbacks, NY, 1998, p. 60.

54. James R. Averill, "Studies of Anger and Aggression: Implications for Theories of Emotion," *American Psychologist*, 1983, Vol. 38, pp. 1145-1160.

55. Lee Goldman, Ph.D., and David A. Haaga, Ph.D., "Depression and the Experience and Expression of Anger in Marital and Other Relationships," *Journal of Nervous Mental Disease*, 1995, Vol. 183, pp. 505-509.

56. David Mace, *Love and Anger in Marriage*, Grand Rapids, MI, Zondervan, 1982 as quoted in Redford Williams, M.D. and Virginia Williams, Ph.D., *Anger Kills: 17 Strategies for Controlling the Hostility that Can Harm Your Health*, Harper Paperbacks, NY, 1998, p. 61.

57. Mary Kay Biaggio, "Clinical Dimensions of Anger Management," *American Journal of Psychotherapy*, No. 41, 1987, pp. 417-427.

58. June Price Tangney, et al., "Assessing Individual Differences in Constructive Versus Destructive Responses to Anger Across the Lifespan," *Journal of Personality and Social Psychology*, 1996, Vol. 70, No. 4, pp. 780-796.

59. Raymond W. Novaco, "The Functions and Regulation of the Arousal of Anger," *American Journal of Psychiatry*, Oct. 1976, Vol. 133, No. 10, pp. 1124-1128.

60. John Lee with Bill Stott, *Facing the Fire: Experiencing and Expressing Anger Appropriately*, Bantam Doubleday Dell Publishers, N.Y., 1995, pp. 138-139.

Chapter 7—Handling Your Anger, Part 1

61. Carol Tavris, *Anger: The Misunderstood Emotion*, Simon & Schuster, New York, 1989, 2 ed., p. 130.

62. David Augsburger, *Caring Enough to Confront, How to Understand and Express Your Deepest Feelings Towards Others*, Regal Books, Glendale, CA, 1980.

63. David Augsburger, *Caring Enough to Confront, How to Understand and Express Your Deepest Feelings Towards Others*, Regal Books, Glendale, CA, 1980, p. 25.

Chapter 8—Handling Your Anger, Part 2

64. Drs. Henry Cloud & John Townsend, *Boundaries: When to Say Yes, When to Say No*, Zondervan Publishing House, Grand Rapids, MI, 1992; Drs. Henry Cloud & John Townsend, *Boundaries with Kids: When to Say Yes, When to Say No*, Zondervan Publishing House, Grand Rapids, MI, 1998.

65. James W. Pennebaker, Ph.D., *Opening Up: The Healing Power of Confiding in Others*, William Morrow & Company, Inc., N.Y., 1990.

66. James W. Pennebaker, et al., "Disclosure of Traumas and Immune Function: Health Implications for Psychotherapy," *Journal of Consulting and Clinical Psychology*, 1988, Vol. 56, No. 2, pp. 139-245; William E. Whitehead, et al., "Anxiety

and Anger in Hypertension," *Journal of Psychosomatic Research,* 1977, Vol. 21, pp. 383-389.

67. James W. Pennebaker, Ph.D.., *Opening Up: The Healing Power of Confiding in Others,* William Morrow & Company, Inc., N.Y., 1990.

68. Howard Kassinove, Ph.D., ABPP, (Editor), *Anger Disorders: Definition, Diagnosis, and Treatment,* Taylor & Francis, Publishers, Washington, D.C., 1995, pp. 120-127.

69. David Augsburger, *Caring Enough to Confront, How to Understand and Express Your Deepest Feelings Towards Others,* Regal Books, Glendale, CA, 1980, pp. 8, 13.

70. Carol Tavris, *Anger: The Misunderstood Emotion,* Simon & Schuster, New York, 1989, 2d ed., p. 290.

71. June Price Tangney, et al., "Assessing Individual Differences in Constructive Versus Destructive Responses to Anger Across the Lifespan," *Journal of Personality and Social Psychology,* 1996, Vol. 70, No. 4, pp. 780-796.

72. Os Guinness, *In Two Minds,* InterVarsity Press, Downers Grove, IL, 1976, p. 207.

73. Carol Tavris, *Anger: The Misunderstood Emotion,* Simon & Schuster, New York, 1989, 2d ed., p. 293.

Chapter 9—Practice What You Know

74. Margaret A. Chesney, Ph.D. and Ray H. Rosenman, M.D., eds. *Anger and Hostility in Cardiovascular and Behavioral Disorders,* Hemisphere Publishing Corporation, WA, 1985, p. 163.

75. Dr. David A. Seamands, "Satan's Deadliest Psychological Weapon," *Healing Our Human Hurts,* Tape Ministers, Pasadena, CA.

76. Martin E. P. Seligman, *Helplessness: On Depression, Development, and Death,* W. H. Freeman and Company, N.Y., 1975.

Chapter 10—Preventing Anger

77. This theme of hidden expectations is described more fully by Clifford J. Segar, M.D., in *Marriage Contracts and Couple Therapy: Hidden Forces in Intimate Relationships,* Brunner/Mazel Publishers, N.Y., 1976.

78. David Augsburger, *Caring Enough to Confront: How to Understand and Express Your Deepest Feelings Toward Others,* Regal Books, Glendale, CA, p. 24.

79. Ann C. Anderson, Ph.D., "Environmental Factors and Aggressive Behavior," *Journal of Clinical Psychiatry,* July 1982, Vol. 43, No. 7, pp. 280-283.

80. Redford Williams, M.D. and Virginia Williams, Ph.D., *Anger Kills: 17 Strategies for Controlling the Hostility that Can Harm Your Health,* Harper Paperbacks, NY,

1998, p. 64; Wolfgang Linden, et al., "Social Determinants of Experienced Anger," *Journal of Behavior Medicine*, Oct. 1997, Vol. 20, No. 5, pp. 415-432.

81. Carol Tavris, *Anger: The Misunderstood Emotion*, Simon & Schuster, New York, 1989, 2d ed., pp. 291-293.

82. Jo Anne Grunbaum, et al., "The Association Between Anger and Hostility and Risk Factors for Coronary Heart Disease in Children and Adolescents: A Review," *Annuals of Behavior Medicine*, 1997, Vol. 19, No. 2, pp. 179-189; Charles Pernini, et al., "Suppressed Aggression Accelerates Early Development of Essential Hypertension," *Journal of Hypertension*, 1991, Vol. 9, pp. 499-503.

Chapter 12—Handling Anger in a Christlike Way

83. Archibald D. Hart, *Feeling Free: Effective Ways to Make Your Emotions Work for You*, Fleming H. Revell Company, Old Tappan, NJ, 1979, p. 85.

Also by Dwight L. Carlson

Why Do Christians Shoot Their Wounded? (InterVarsity Press)